More
AbraVocabra

The Amazingly
Sensible Approach
to Teaching Vocabulary

M.S.D. Samston

Cottonwood Press, Inc.

Fort Collins, Colorado

Cottonwood Press, Inc.
107 Cameron Drive
Fort Collins, CO 80525

www.cottonwoodpress.com

1-800-864-4297

ISBN 1-877673-53-6

Printed in the United States of America

Table of Contents

AbraVocabra Basics

Note: *More AbraVocabra* is a sequel to the popular book *AbraVocabra*. Both books follow the same principles and format but contain different word lists and different games.

Helping students improve their vocabularies is a project with enormous benefits. When students improve their vocabularies, they feel smarter. They find themselves understanding more of what they read and what they hear. They find it easier to express themselves because they have a better command of their language. They feel more powerful because, indeed, they are more powerful.

Luckily, vocabulary improvement is a relatively easy project for the classroom, and one that reaps results almost immediately. The books *AbraVocabra* and *More AbraVocabra* make vocabulary study easy, interesting, practical and, yes, even enjoyable!

The methods described in *AbraVocabra* and *More AbraVocabra* are based on two fundamental ideas:

1. Vocabulary study should be based on common words, not obscure words that students will encounter only once or twice in a lifetime.

2. Vocabulary is not the same as spelling.

Common words. Vocabulary study is too often focused on unusual words encountered in novels, short stories or other materials students are reading in class. Just because the words "pasquinade" or "saloop" occur in a story doesn't mean that most people need to know them. Certainly, a teacher should point out the meanings in the context of the story, but having students memorize definitions of words they are unlikely to encounter again is a waste of time.

The words in *AbraVocabra* and *More AbraVocabra* are real-world words, words that anyone is likely to read in a newspaper, hear on the news, read in a magazine. In fact, just seeing and hearing the words outside the classroom reinforces for students the idea that the words are useful and important ones to know.

Vocabulary vs. spelling. Too often, schools lump vocabulary and spelling together. On vocabulary tests, teachers require students to know the correct spelling, as well as the meaning, of the words.

The problem is that learning to spell and learning the meaning of a word are two different processes. You can learn to spell something without knowing its meaning, just as you can learn a word's meaning without having any idea how to spell it. That doesn't mean that knowing both isn't a good idea. It just means that one is neither dependent on nor necessary for the other.

Imagine teaching an auto repair class. If your goal is to teach auto repair, you probably aren't going to require students to spell every part of the engine correctly. Teaching spelling along with auto repair would only slow everyone down.

With vocabulary study, it is important to ask, "What am I trying to teach here, anyway? What is my goal?" If your goal is to help your students expand their vocabularies as much as possible, then it is not a good idea to require them to know how to spell each vocabulary word they learn.

Before English teachers everywhere have heart attacks at such heresy, a bit of clarification is in order. You should still *encourage* students to learn how to spell the words and, in fact, you should *require* correct spelling of the words whenever students use them. However, it is important to allow them to refer to the correct spelling, as needed. (With many students, just getting them to copy a word correctly is a big step in the right direction!)

Don't worry about parents or other teachers criticizing you for being too easy on the kids. You aren't being easy on them. Your goal is to build powerful vocabularies and to help your students expand their vocabularies as much as they possibly can. Teaching spelling will vastly slow down your progress. Explain your position. It is a perfectly justifiable one.

The truth is that people need to recognize and understand far more words than they ever need to be able to spell. If your goal is to help students learn as many new words as possible, take spelling out of the equation.

Using this Book

More AbraVocabra takes a practical approach to vocabulary study. Each of the 24 lists is made up of 10 practical words that anyone is likely to encounter in reading the newspaper, listening to the news or reading magazines. They are all useful words to know.

Students are not overwhelmed with long, impossible-looking lists. They receive 10 words at a time, with two bonus words thrown in. They study the words for 2-3 weeks at a time, using only a small amount of class time. If students study and learn all 24 lists over the course of a year, they will have learned 240 new words. Of course, you can easily do fewer lists, or even add your own words to the lists included in the book.

Here is the approach, in a nutshell, followed by a more detailed explanation of each step:

1. Have students guess the meaning of the words.

2. Have students "play" with the words, using them in a variety of activities.

3. Test students.

4. Review by playing Vocabra after every fourth set of words.

Have students guess the meaning of the words. Each word in a *More AbraVocabra* list includes two "tip-off" sentences. The tip-off sentences show the words in context and include clues as to their meaning. Read these sentences aloud or put them on the chalkboard or overhead. (If you're particularly creative or simply enjoy the thrill of ad-libbing, make up your own sentences right on the spot instead.) Let students try to guess the meaning of each word and come up with a correct definition on their own.

This "figuring out" step is very important. It puts students in an active role rather than a passive one of sitting back and receiving the answers from you or mindlessly copying dictionary definitions they often don't understand.

Students need definitions that make sense to them. The lists in *More AbraVocabra* include simple definitions to use as a guideline. However, it is important to remember that only one or two common definitions are included for each word. Students who become familiar with one meaning can later learn other meanings of a word.

The main purpose of the tip-off sentences is to give students a context for remembering words. It is also helpful to share stories or helpful hints. For example, one teacher always tells this story about the word "erroneous":

> *My college roommate Ruth was in a car accident. My boyfriend and I rushed to the hospital. The hospital staff wouldn't give information unless we were relatives, so my boyfriend quickly identified himself as Ruth's brother. Later, he was paged to sign some papers. Of course, he didn't want to sign the papers, so he told the nurse, "I'm afraid you have received some erroneous information about my relationship to Ruth." The nurse looked at him blankly. "Huh?" He repeated himself. She looked at him blankly again. Finally, he realized that she didn't know what "erroneous" meant. "The information was false," he said. "There's a misunderstanding. I'm afraid I'm not Ruth's brother."*

After that story, virtually all the students remember the definition, especially when the teacher also points out that the word "error" is almost entirely imbedded in "erroneous." Giving the students a context for the words helps them learn the words easily.

Have students start "playing" with the words. Spend anywhere from one to four weeks working on a given list of words with your students. You shouldn't have to take much class time for this, but students won't mind the time you do spend. In fact, your students will probably find themselves enjoying vocabulary study. The chapter "Playing with Vocabulary Words" (page 11) in *More AbraVocabra* contains dozens of activities to help students get involved with their vocabulary words and use them. Use one or more of these activities for each list of words.

Test the students. When it seems that students know the words, schedule a test. (A test is included after each word list.) The test itself will be an activity that helps reinforce the words. For most students, the test will be a positive experience, for they will know the words and do well. Each test requires students to use the words and encourages them to be creative in finding ways to incorporate the bonus words into the test stories.

Review. After every four lists, play the Vocabra Game with your students to review and reinforce the words they have learned. (See directions on pages 24–26.)

Addressing a Few Questions

Why aren't the words listed by grade level? How do I know where to start my students? The *More AbraVocabra* word lists are not divided into "sixth grade words" or "ninth grade words." That's because useful words are just that — useful words. The words included in this book are words that any reasonably educated person is likely to know.

How do you know if a list fits your students? Ask them. Read the words, one word at a time, and have students show by a raise of their hands if they know the word. This shouldn't take more than five minutes. No, it won't be highly scientific and accurate. Yes, a few kids will probably lie and say they know words that they don't know, and some will pretend not to know words that they know perfectly well. Still, you will get an idea about the appropriateness of the list. In a typical junior high or middle school classroom, most students will know fewer than half the words. (Don't worry if there is a word here and there that you don't know either. All of us have gaps in our knowledge.)

What about the students who know most or all of the words? Students who know most of a word list can have a different challenge, still within the framework of the class. Challenge them to come up with their own individual lists of words, using books, magazines, newspapers and other people (including you) for ideas. These students can receive extra credit for being tested on the regular class list *and* their own list.

No, you don't need to write extra tests. Give the students a real challenge by having them complete the same test as the other students, then continuing the test story so that all of their personal vocabulary words are used in a way that shows their meaning. Students who already have strong vocabularies will usually enjoy the creativity involved in adapting the test for their own purposes.

Students with their own lists can do most of the same activities as the rest of the class, but using different words. (For group activities, have them stick with the standard class list. They may not want to be singled out.) Students who know most, but not all, of the words in a list should use substitutions for only the words they already know.

How do you keep students honest with all this? You can't. However, you can try appealing to the "best and honest" part of them by encouraging them to substitute words when they already know some of them on a list. Point out that, yes, anyone can take the easy route and study words he already knows. However, he will gain nothing. He will be wasting time and going nowhere. Sometimes appealing to the best in students has surprising results, especially with vocabulary. Students quickly sense for themselves the power of new words, the feeling of understanding more, of feeling smarter — and they plunge ahead with enthusiasm.

What if my students know what a word means but use it in a strange way?
Students don't usually start off doing anything perfectly, and that applies to using new words

as well. When teaching vocabulary, imagine concentric learning circles. There are phases involved in improving vocabulary.

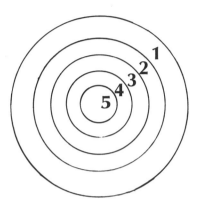

Steps in Making a Word Part of Your Vocabulary

1. **Noticing a word.** Before you start to learn a word, you need to notice it. Quite often, the brain just skips over words that are unfamiliar.

2. **Getting a general sense of the word's meaning.** You may start recognizing that a word is generally positive or generally negative, or that it has something to do with astronomy, for example.

3. **Getting a clearer sense of its meaning.** The meaning becomes more sharply focused. While you still might not use the word yourself, you understand what it means, especially in context.

4. **Being able to use the word in a way that is generally appropriate.** When you first start using a new word, you may not use it quite correctly. You haven't learned the nuances of meaning, the prepositions usually associated with it, etc. However, you are getting there. (Little children may say "Want juice" before they learn to say, "I want some juice, please." That's okay. They don't have everything down pat, but that will come.)

5. **Learning the subtleties of using the word correctly.** More experience will lead to more appropriate use of the word. When you have learned the meaning of a word you will also, typically, start seeing it everywhere. Seeing it in other contexts will help you learn how to use the word appropriately.

Correct spelling of the word can occur at any of the five stages above — or not at all. Even people who can use a word correctly may still need to look it up in a dictionary in order to spell it correctly.

Does all this work? Yes. Here is what some teachers have said about the methods and ideas described in *AbraVocabra*, this book's predecessor:

Addressing a Few Questions

- "My students started coming back to me after ninth grade achievement tests and saying, 'Hey, did you take our vocabulary words from the achievement tests? The tests were just full of them!' Well, of course I didn't. The words on the lists are just sensible words, and I suppose a lot of them may be on the achievement tests. I don't know. I do know that the kids were pretty pleased to feel so confident about how they did on at least one section of the test!"

- "After a few weeks of vocabulary study, my students always start saying, 'That word we learned is all over the place! I keep hearing it on TV and reading it in different places. How did you know it was going to start showing up everywhere?' I didn't know. It's just that once they learn a word, they start becoming aware of it. The word was appearing all along, but they didn't see it. Now that they know it, they are aware of it."

- "Vocabulary study has become such a positive thing in my classroom. When my principal observed me last year, my ninth graders were actually arguing about who should read his or her vocabulary story first. They were so excited, and my principal was impressed that I could get them excited about words."

- "I know our vocabulary study has been successful when my students start defining new vocabulary words with vocabulary words we have studied in the past. It always happens when I use this approach."

- "Vocabulary tests are something my kids actually look forward to! They all get a chance to do well, and the tests themselves often have them smiling and using their own creativity. Tests days are a real 'upper'!"

The key to learning new words is using them. Try some or all of the activity ideas that follow, choosing two or three activities for each word list. You don't need to spend a lot of time. You do need to get the students involved.

Playing with Vocabulary Words

As students do the various activities, take time to discuss how words can take different forms — for example, *scruples, scrupulous, unscrupulous* or *squalid* and *squalor*. As they come up, discuss word roots and their meanings and how they can help in figuring out the meaning of a word (Example: philo=love, anthro=man, philanthropist=a person who loves people and wants to increase their well-being, especially by charitable aid or donations).

The activities that follow are very successful in helping students learn new vocabulary words.

Story Time

One of the most effective ways to get students to play with words is to have them put all the words in a vocabulary list into a story. This is a fairly sophisticated task, requiring students to understand the meanings of the words well enough to find a framework for them, thus relating all the words in some way.

Some students may not be able to do it. If they can't, allow them to use any "leftover" words in separate sentences that show their meaning. For young students, in fact, you may want to have them combine only two words at a time in a sentence or short paragraph.

Take time now and then to let students share their stories. They enjoy having an audience for their work, and some students will go to great lengths to create funny, entertaining stories — if they know their peers might hear them.

More challenges. Vary the story assignment in as many ways as possible. Give students some of these challenges, a different one each time:

- See how short you can make the story.

- Make the whole story about *one* of the following subjects: sports, cats or telephones.

- Write a story that includes *all* of the following subjects: sports, cats or telephones. Of course, you may use any other topics as well. See the following page for a few topic ideas for vocabulary stories.

    Possibilities for topics are endless. In fact, you might even want to have students write topic ideas on slips of paper. (Suggest that they choose interesting, specific nouns. "Pizza" is more interesting and specific than "food," for example.) Collect the slips of paper and put them in a jar. Then draw three topics for students to use in their stories. Save the jar and draw three different topics the next time you assign a story.

Playing with Vocabulary Words

A few possible story topics:

fast food restaurants	grandparents	the Empire State Building
football	spiders	ferry boats
MTV	cars	straws
the Internet	vacations	coffee
computers	in-line skates	colds
skate boards	extreme sports	taxis
subways	boats	crayons
pollution	amusement park rides	Darth Vader
sandals	movies	video games
parents	Egypt	lacrosse
puppies	kites	Will Smith
socks	jeans	commercials
CDs	sisters	GI Joe dolls
teeth	brothers	tractors
birthdays	the Chicago Bulls	lawn mowers
love	ice cream	canned peaches
George Washington	broccoli	telephones
lunch	summer jobs	lime green
volleyball	pizza	the Fourth of July
dragons	war	money
spinach	buffalo	crushes
friends	tuna	allergies
cartoons	lighthouses	shopping
basketball	spaghetti and meatballs	flutes
chocolate	the alphabet	coconut cream pie
Sunday	tricycles	lockers
apples	Jell-O	the Olympics
mountains	the Grand Canyon	bouquet of roses

• One more idea is to have students write something other than a story, using the vocabulary words. Some examples: an acceptance speech, a lecture from a parent, a love letter, a commercial for a product, a letter of complaint or a newspaper article.

Grading tips. Vocabulary stories can be very easy to grade. Be sure to have students underline each word used. Then scan the stories quickly. If all the words are used in a sensible way, allow the full amount of points.

Another method is to assign two criteria for grading — for example, *using the vocabulary words correctly* and *having no run-on sentences*. Another time the criteria might be *using the vocabulary words correctly* and *having no spelling errors* (or *no sentence fragments* or *no errors in capitalization* or something else).

Choose a simple grading method that fits your style and your classroom. Don't turn the vocabulary stories into a huge pile of work for yourself. Just the act of doing the stories is the valuable part of the activity. In fact, sometimes you might not even want to grade the stories at all.

Oral Stories

A quick three to five minute lesson involves having students use the words orally. Have someone start a story, using as many words from the vocabulary list as possible in one minute. (Remind students that the story must indicate the word's meaning in some way.) Have someone else continue the story for a minute, and then someone else, for another minute. See how many words the class members can use, total, in three minutes.

Quickie Skits

Break the students into small groups of about five students each. Give the groups 10 minutes to come up with a short skit that uses as many vocabulary words as possible. (Of course, they act out the skits in front of the class.)

Acting Out the Meaning

At the end of class when you've got three minutes to spare, ask someone to volunteer to act out the meaning of a word. For example, someone might act out "rotund" by holding out her hands and imitating a round stomach.

Another idea is to give a volunteer (or volunteers) a situation to act out, using at least three vocabulary words in the performance. For example, you might give a student this situation to act out using the words "gawk," "grotesque" and "bicker": an irate customer talks to the stylist about her terrible haircut.

A few more ideas for situations follow:

- At a supermarket, a chatty checker talks on and on and on.
- A convenience store manager hates kids and starts trying to get a group of them to leave the second they come into the store.
- An enthusiastic coach encourages her team.
- A teenager talks on the phone to her best friend.
- A parent lectures his son, who has come home five hours late.
- A mother can't get her baby to stop crying.
- A school bus breaks down five miles from school.
- A singer loses his voice during a performance.
- Two best friends say goodbye because one is moving away.
- A candidate running for office promises a free car to all sixteen-year-olds.
- Two business owners discuss ways to promote their bowling alley.

- Ice skaters arrive at a pond, only to find that the ice has melted.

- Three people on a diet decide what to have for lunch.

- Picnickers are plagued by ants.

- Three friends decide to start their own band.

- A student is afraid to show her parents her report card.

- A father drags his seven-year-old to the dentist.

- Parents explain to their children that the family won't be going to Disney World after all.

- A gardener shows off the 35-pound cantaloupe she grew in her garden.

- A ten-year-old finds a wallet full of hundred dollar bills.

- Three young people discover a time machine.

- A rock star performs before a huge audience, but the audience is not pleased.

- A waiter at a restaurant brings an irritable customer the wrong plate of food.

- A car stalls at a stop sign, and frustrated drivers are trapped in their car for eight blocks.

- Two actors try to do a commercial for "Zippy Dippy Drink," which they discover is an awful-tasting combination of carrot and spinach juice.

Drawing

See if students can draw the meaning of a word, using the word itself. Have them open their minds to all kinds of possibilities. Here are a couple of examples:

rotund

macabre

Another idea is to assign a specific vocabulary word to each student. Then ask students to draw a picture that somehow illustrates their word, but without using the word itself in the illustration. (For example, a student might illustrate "gawk" by drawing someone with her eyeballs bulging.) The class as a whole then tries to guess which vocabulary word is illustrated by each picture.

Vocabulary Bee

To review words, have a vocabulary bee, conducted somewhat like a spelling bee. In a vocabulary bee, the class is divided into two teams. Unlike a spelling bee, however, students aren't eliminated from the game when they miss a word.

Because students will probably know most of the words, it's a good idea to add question "levels," to make the game more interesting. Let each student select a one, two or three point question. For one-point questions, students simply define the word correctly and earn their team a point. For two-point questions, they must define the word correctly and use it in a sentence. Three point questions require the student to define two words correctly and use both in one sentence that indicates their meaning.

Categories

After your class has studied four or five word lists, have students work in small groups to categorize the words, placing at least three words in each category. Students should come up with their own categories.

There are, of course, no limits to the number and kind of categories students might choose. Just a few examples: "adjectives," "words that begin with *t*," "words that describe someone who is mad," "words good for describing food," "words that would be perfect for a horror story," "three-letter words," "words used to describe someone negatively," "words that might be used by a doctor," etc.

Try not to give the groups any hints. Insist that the students themselves determine the categories, and remind them that there is no one right answer to the exercise. As long as the category has at least three words and the words fit the category, the answer is correct.

This exercise really requires creative thinking and a strong understanding of the words. It is an excellent activity for review.

A Novel Approach

Ask students to apply their vocabulary words to a novel (or short story) they are reading in class. A few examples: Moby Dick was a whale of *gargantuan* proportions. Daisy Miller was a *vivacious* young woman who was always into one thing or another. Miss Havisham was a *haughty* woman whom no one liked.

Journal Topics

If your students keep class journals, have them pick words from the vocabulary list that definitely *do* and definitely *do not* describe themselves. Ask them to elaborate.

Sell It

Divide the class into small groups, and give each group one of the assigned vocabulary words. Ask the group to imagine being an ad agency hired to sell the word to the rest of the class. Give students a short time to come up with an idea for a commercial or an advertisement that will show the word's usefulness and meaning.

Dialogue

Ask students to write a short two or three-person dialogue (conversation) using all the words on the vocabulary list. Or have them design a short comic strip that includes all the words. (The dialogue, of course, goes in the "bubbles.")

Newspaper Captions

Cut out several newspaper or magazine photographs. Ask students to come up with captions that include the vocabulary words and describe what might be happening in each photograph.

Write a Poem

Challenge students to write a short, two to four line rhyming poem for each word. Example:

Mom was indignant.
My father was mad.
I got grounded,
and I was sad.

Song Titles

Have students write titles of songs, movies, TV shows and/or books that include one or more of their vocabulary words. Some examples:

- "I Was *Indignant*, so I Ran Over His Lawn Mower With My Truck" — a country-western song
- *The Indignant Princess: A Story of Revenge* — a book

Sports Reports

Have students act as sports reporters, covering a sporting event of their choice. Each story should include all the vocabulary words. (Or allow students to write two or three short sports stories in order to use all the words.)

Setting up a Bonus System

Making vocabulary study — except for tests — an "extra" or a "bonus" often brings amazing results. Students who don't care much about doing the required work will work very hard for anything labeled "bonus." The system described below can have very positive results.

This bonus point system involves keeping a running total of bonus points on a chart for each class. Announce that whenever the bonus points reach a certain amount (say 300 or 500 points), the class will have a game day, with prizes. (See pages 18–21 for a game that works very well for game days. The games require thinking and involve words. Most kids enjoy them.)

Explain that bonus points are arbitrary, given and taken away according to your judgment or even your whim. You might give five bonus points one day for having someone define a word correctly. You might take two away another day because three students kept shouting out answers. Explain that you are the bonus point queen, king, dictator — whatever term you can dream up to fit. Do this with good humor, and keep it light. Don't turn bonus points into something that seems too much like grades.

Be free with your bonus points, and vary the amount you grant. Here are just a few ideas for using them:

- Take three minutes at the beginning of class and give a bonus point for each correct definition given as you call on different students. (You might even want to set a timer.)

- Another day, announce that you will give 10 class bonus points for anyone who can define all 10 vocabulary words, quickly. Ask for volunteers, or call on someone.

- Give two points to each student who uses a designated vocabulary word correctly in a sentence that shows the word's meaning. You might do two or three words at the beginning or end of class each day.

- Make students aware that you will give bonus points at any time, even out of the classroom. Call on students in the halls. Arrange for the principal to call a student to the office during homeroom and ask him what "homogenous" means. During an assembly, announce that you will give 10 bonus points to your third period English class if Alfred can define "infinitesimal." (Be sure to choose someone who can take the heat.)

- Tell kids you will take five minutes every now and then for reporting on "word sightings." If Dan Rather says "indignant" on the nightly news, give two points to the student who reports as much. If someone brings in a newspaper article with "erroneous" in it, allow a point or two.

- Make the point-giving truly subjective and random. Some days, if you are feeling generous, give 25 points for a simple question. On another day, give one point for a fairly hard question.

- With each test, keep a record of words that everyone in the class got right. Hang this list of words that your class "owns" on the wall and add to it each week. Give five bonus points for every "owned" word.

- Tell students that bonus points are just that — bonus. You can give them or take them away. If someone wants to argue loudly about something and disrupt the class, just quietly take away two points, then — if necessary — another two. You don't have to say much. Students will get the point. Best of all, they won't usually support the student who is disruptive. Handled lightly and with good humor, this technique can help your students behave, as well as help them learn vocabulary.

- The following games (pages 18–21) make an excellent reward for students earning enough bonus points for a game day.

Name _____

For each category listed along the left side of the page, think of an appropriate word that begins with the letter at the top of the column. The first item is done for you.

	Things to wear	Things you might find in a kitchen	6-letter words	Names of TV shows	Toys
D	dresses				
I					
C					
T					
I					
O					
N					
A					
R					
Y					

Name _____

For each category listed along the left side of the page, think of an appropriate word that begins with the letter at the top of the column. The first item is done for you.

	Things advertised in commercials	Sandwich ingredients	Things that fly	Verbs	Words that are related to sports
A	Alka Seltzer				
L					
P					
H					
A					
B					
E					
T					

Name _____

For each category listed along the left side of the page, think of an appropriate word that begins with the letter at the top of the column. The first item is done for you.

	Colors	Girls' names	Parts of an automobile	5-letter adjectives	Kinds of candy
C	cream				
O					
N					
S					
O					
N					
A					
N					
T					
S					

More AbraVocabra • © 2001 Cottonwood Press, Inc. • www.cottonwoodpress.com • 800-864-4297 • Fort Collins, Colorado
20

For each category listed along the left side of the page, think of an appropriate word that begins with the letter at the top of the column. The first item is done for you.

	V	**O**	**W**	**E**	**L**	**S**
Things that can make a teacher irate	*vandalized desks*					
7-letter words						
Animals						
Careers and jobs						
Category you choose						
Something a person can usually buy at a mall						
Boys' names						
Cartoon characters						

Possible answers to bonus games:

	D	I	C	T	I	O	N	A	R	Y
Items of clothing	dresses	infant onesie	capri pants	tuxedo	Isotoner gloves	oxfords	neck tie	anklets	romper	yar-mulke
Things you might find in a kitchen	dishwasher	ice maker	cutting board	toaster	ice tongs	oven	napkins	after-dinner mints	refrigera-tor	yams
6-letter words	direct	intend	colors	talons	indigo	office	nation	aspens	runner	yellow
Names of TV shows	Dawson's Creek	I Love Lucy	Charmed	Temptation Island	I Dream of Jeannie	Oprah	NYPD Blue	Angel	Roswell	Young and the Restless
Toys	dump truck	inline skates	chalk	Tonka truck	inflatable pool	Operation	Nerf ball	action figures	Risk	yo-yo

	A	L	P	H	A	B	E	T
Things advertised in commercials	Alka Seltzer	Listerine	Pampers	hash-browns	apple juice	Band-aids	E*Trade	Tide
Sandwich ingredients	albacore tuna	lettuce	pickles	ham	aged Cheddar	bread	egg	tomato
Things that fly	airplane	ladybug	pizza dough	horsefly	arrow	baton	eagle	time
Verbs	advance	limp	panic	harm	alternate	beseech	elect	tremor
Words that are related to sports	athlete	lacrosse	punt	helmet	arena	bases	exercise	touch-down

C O N S O N A N T S

	C	O	N	S	O	N	A	N	T	S
Colors	cream	orange	navy blue	salmon	olive green	nutmeg	amber	nectarine	tan	silver
Girls' names	Carly	Opal	Nadine	Selma	Olivia	Nellie	Adena	Nora	Teresa	Susan
Parts of an automobile	clutch	odometer	new tires	spark plugs	oil filter	neutral safety switch	automatic transmission	nuts and bolts	timing belt	shocks
5-letter adjectives	clean	obese	noisy	slimy	oafish	nutty	awful	nerdy	testy	sharp
Kinds of candy	caramel	O'Henry	Nerds	Snickers	orange slices	Nutty Bar	Atomic Fireballs	Nestle's Crunch	Twix	Snocaps

V O W E L S

	Things that can make a teacher irate	7-letter words	Animals	Careers and jobs	Category you choose (places I'd like to go)	Something a person can usually buy at a mall	Boys' names	Cartoon characters
S	smart alecs	surpass	skunk	singer	South America	shoes	Sylvester	Scooby Doo
L	loud yelling in the halls	legends	lion	lifeguard	London	lizard	Leopold	Lisa Simpson
E	evening phone calls	element	elephant	electrical engineer	Ellis Island	earrings	Ethan	Elroy
O	obnoxious behavior	offense	orangutan	oil baron	Orlando	Orange Julius	Oscar	Olive Oyl
W	withering looks	whistle	whale	waitress	Washington, D.C.	wool socks	William	Wilma Flintstone
V	vandalized desks	vaccine	vampire bat	vice principal	Vienna	videos	Victor	Veronica

Directions to Vocabra Game

Overview

With Vocabra, teams compete against each other to define vocabulary words correctly. They earn or lose points, according to point values they themselves decide to risk for each round. Words are selected through random drawings, so students never know which words they will be asked to define.

The teams consist of two student teams and a third "team" made up of just the teacher. It is possible for either student team *or* the teacher to win the game. Of course, the finer points of the game help make it more interesting. These are outlined below.

Preparation

1. There is a Vocabra game card located after every fourth word list. Photocopy the card containing the words your class is currently studying. Make a transparency of it for the overhead projector. (It is also possible to draw the game card on the chalkboard, if you don't have access to an overhead. Another possibility is to photocopy the game card and give each student a copy.)

2. Photocopy page 137 and cut apart the numbers and letters on the copy. Put the number slips in a "number jar" and the letter slips in a "letter jar." (Okay, it could also be a box. Or a paper bag. Or a sock.) Note that "A1" and "A2" refer to the first and second "A"s that spell out "Vocabra" on the cards.

3. Have a clock, timer or watch readily accessible.

4. Divide the class into two equally sized teams and have the teams sit on separate sides of the room. Determine a "play order" for each team — usually left to right, or front to back along the rows.

5. Draw three columns on the chalkboard for recording scores. Head two of the columns with the teams' names (or Team A, Team B). Head the third column "Teacher."

Playing the Game

1. Explain that, once play begins, the game will continue for exactly 30 minutes. When the timer sounds, the game is over, no matter what is happening at that time. The team with the most points at that time is the winner. Point out that either team or you, the teacher, can be the winner of the game. (In fact, it's fun to make an agreement ahead of time about the prizes for the winners. As the teacher, you can have some fun with what your prize might be. Be creative!)

2. Give a brief overview of the game: Vocabra is played in rounds. A "risk taker" from one team decides how many points he is going to risk (from 5–50 points, in increments of 5), without knowing which word on the game board he will be asked to define. If he defines the word correctly, his team will earn the amount of points he has risked. If he misses the word, his team will lose the amount of points he has risked, and the opposing team will have a chance to define the word and earn the points. If both teams miss the word, the teacher gets the points. (That's how the teacher earns points — when neither team can define a word.) The next round begins with a risk taker from the other team.

   Point out that you, the teacher, will make the final determination on the correctness of a definition. Explain that you are looking for reasonably clear explanations of what a word means, not dictionary definitions. If a student's definition is not quite clear enough, though not *wrong*, you may ask her to use it in a sentence, for clarification.

   Also point out that the rules of Vocabra give the teacher another power: subtracting points for excessive rowdiness or rudeness (five points at a time works well) and for shouting out the correct definition to a word. Explain that you will not award points when someone on a team shouts the definition to the risk taker.

Example. Assume that you have flipped a coin and determined that Team A will play first. The first risk taker in the play order for that team is Joe, who decides to risk 25 points.

A member of the other team then draws a slip from the letter jar and a slip from the number jar — in this case a C and an 8. That means the location of Joe's word is C-8 on the Vocabra Card. The teams are using the first Vocabra Card on page 45, so Joe's word is *egotistical*. (Note: After being drawn, the slips go back in the number and letter jars. In future rounds, it's possible that C and 8 can be drawn again.)

Joe then has 30 seconds to give an accurate definition of *egotistical*. If he does so, his team earns 25 points. If he can't do so, his team loses 25 points. (Yes, negative scores are possible.) Play then goes to Team B, and the next person on Team B gets a chance at defining the word. If she defines *egotistical* correctly, her team earns 25 points. If she misses it, however, her team does *not* lose points. (After all, her team didn't decide how much to risk.) Instead, the 25 points go to the teacher.

After the points risked have been recorded on the chalkboard (whether to Team A, Team B or the teacher), the next round begins with Team B, even though a Team B player had the last chance at a definition. That's because the initial risk taker for each round alternates between Team A and Team B.

3. Some of the factors that make the game interesting are these:

    *   Along with the regular vocabulary words, bonus words appear on each Vocabra card, as well as eight "weird words" — words that are unusual or strange-sounding and not widely known. Students need to remember, when they choose the number of points they will risk, that they might wind up with *any* of these words.

    *   When neither team knows the definition of a word, the teacher gives the definition (The definitions for the "weird words" appear in the Appendix, page 138.) Students are advised to pay attention because the same word could come up again.

    *   Risk takers are, in a sense, "betting" on the likelihood that they will know a word. It is important for them to remember that they can *lose* points for their teams as well as gain points.

    *   Chance plays a big part in the game. Words are selected at random, by drawing the number and letter slips from the jars. Sometimes the "weird words" will come up again and again. Sometimes they won't be selected at all. No one knows what words will be selected in a drawing.

One final note. Have fun with Vocabra. The point is to help students review and reinforce the words they have learned. The atmosphere should be one of light-hearted competition and risk taking. Take a playful attitude, not a deadly serious one. Enjoy your students. Enjoy the review!

AbraVocabra
Word Lists
1–24

Vocabulary List #1

alternative: a choice or possibility

- There are many **alternatives** to eating peanut butter and banana sandwiches every day for lunch, but Donnie doesn't want to know about them.

- Magda had trouble deciding which career **alternative** was best for her — being a brain surgeon or being a mime.

utopia: a perfect place or ideal situation

- After sound-proofing the walls so he could escape his older brother's daily tuba practice, John considered his room a **utopia**.

- Mel has his own idea of **utopia**: an unlimited supply of teriyaki-flavored beef jerky.

ashen: the gray color of ashes; often used to describe the complexion of someone who has experienced something upsetting or traumatic

- After he was attacked by angry flamingos on his safari, Leon's face was **ashen**.

- Wanda looked **ashen** after the ice cream truck nearly ran over Snuggles, her pet python.

affable: friendly and easy to speak to

- Lester found the secretary much more **affable** than Mr. Sower, the president.

- Rich was always **affable** during television interviews, even when talking to Ty Mondragon, the meanest wrestling champion in the state.

barter: to trade one thing for another without using money

- "The secret to a good relationship with your younger brother is learning to **barter** candy for silence," Rocky told his girlfriend.

- The pastry chef next door often **barters** with Mabel for the use of her riding lawnmower, so her kitchen is always stocked with gourmet cheesecakes and other fine desserts.

exposé: revealed information that may damage someone's reputation

- The **exposé** contained shocking details about golf pro "Squeaky Clean" Jones.

- The new reporter had written an **exposé** about Mr. Earl, the fur coat salesman.

irreverent: disrespectful

- Some kids may seem **irreverent** when they yell in public, but often they just don't know any better.

- Charlie Chase, the top disc jockey in the city, is often **irreverent** about topics that his guests take very seriously.

gala: a fancy celebration

- The **gala** honoring Miss Howard for her donation to the art gallery was held on the large lawn behind the museum.

- Betsy was invited to a **gala** marking the new opera's opening night, but she raised eyebrows by wearing an awful green polyester dress from the 1970s.

ostracize: to shut out or banish

- Kevin wanted to take up tap dancing, but he was afraid of being **ostracized** by his football buddies.

- Marie knew what it felt like to be **ostracized**, so she made a point to talk to the new girl in school when nobody else would.

scapegoat: a person who is forced to take the blame for the mistakes or crimes of others

- Instead of realistically dealing with the issues at hand, the city council members liked to make the mayor the **scapegoat** for the city's problems.

- Colin, the goalie, became the **scapegoat** when the soccer team lost the game.

Bonus Words

★parody: a funny or exaggerated imitation of something

- *Animal House* is film **parody** of life in a college fraternity house.

- As soon as Mr. Johnson left the room, Billy had the other students laughing with his skillful **parody** of the teacher's mannerisms.

★behemoth: something enormous in size

- "That Great Dane looked like a **behemoth** next to my Chihuahua," Miss Gordon observed.

- The largest animal on earth, the blue whale, is definitely a **behemoth**.

Name _____

Test

Matching

Match each word in the left column to its correct definition in the right column.

_____ 1. ashen

_____ 2. exposé

_____ 3. gala

_____ 4. irreverent

_____ 5. utopia

_____ 6. scapegoat

_____ 7. alternative

_____ 8. affable

_____ 9. ostracize

_____ 10. barter

★Bonus words

_____ 11. behemoth

_____ 12. parody

a. to trade one thing for another without using money

b. a fancy celebration

c. disrespectful

d. a funny or exaggerated imitation of something

e. an animal known for burying its head in the sand

f. friendly and easy to speak to

g. a person who is forced to take the blame for the mistakes or crimes of others

h. the gray color of ashes; often used to describe the complexion of someone who has experienced something upsetting or traumatic

i. revealed information that may damage someone's reputation

j. a perfect place or ideal situation

k. a common farm animal

l. something enormous in size

m. an inability to decide between two choices

n. to shut out or banish

o. a choice or possibility

Fill-in-the-Blank

Directions: The first 10 words listed above belong in the story below. Read the story and use the clues in the text to place each word in the correct blank space provided. You may change the form of a word to fit the story, if you need to. (For example, you might need to add *ed, ing, ly* or *s.*)

Elton's Exposé

Elton Lotsabux had everything he wanted: video games, a swimming pool, a dirt bike and all the candy he could eat. The other kids thought that Elton's life was a/an
(1) _____, but he was never happy. Even though his father smiled a lot and was
(2) _____, he was always too tired to play with Elton. Elton threw tantrums and broke his toys just to get attention.

One evening, Mrs. Lotsabux said to her husband, "Something needs to be done about Elton. I'm tired of his tantrums."

"Sure, dear," said Mr. Lotsabux, tapping away at his laptop.

"How about sending him to boot camp?" asked Mrs. Lotsabux.

That got her husband's attention. "Oh no, dear. I think we need to cheer him up with a/an (3) _____ in his honor," he said.

"That's the last thing he needs. He is spoiled rotten. He is just plain (4) _____ to everyone."

The next morning Elton rode his dirt bike into the dining room. "You shouldn't ride that in the house," his mother said. He kept riding around the table. He knew his mother wouldn't punish him because his parents didn't believe in that. Instead, she had to (5) _____ with him, offering a treat in return for his good behavior.

"Elton, if you stop riding your bike in the house, you can have a popsicle," she said. He rode his bike into the kitchen, where he demanded that the maid give him a popsicle.

"Your father thinks we need to have another party in honor of you," the maid said.

"No!" Elton shouted, "I don't want a party. I want to go bowling with my dad!" He ran to the park and sat under a big tree. A woman who worked for the *Daily Scoop*, a tabloid newspaper, walked by. "Hey, you're the son of the famous millionaire, Bartholomew Lotsabux," she said.

"No, I'm not," Elton said. Sometimes he liked to pretend he was the son of a regular guy. "My dad is completely broke. He went bowling with the guys last night. Afterwards they gambled and he lost all of his money," he said.

"Really? Wow! That's terrible!" she said, walking away. "Thanks for the great story, kid."

The next day the *Daily Scoop* ran a cover story with a shocking headline: "Local millionaire in the poor house after gambling disaster." The (6) _____ was printed on the front page and contained many lies. "I'm glad my dad lost his millions," the newspaper quoted Elton as saying. "He's always wanted to run a bowling alley."

When Elton saw the *Daily Scoop* on the kitchen table and read the headline, his face turned (7) _____. "Dad is going to change his mind about punishment now," he thought. "He's going to ground me forever!"

Just then, Elton's dad came into the kitchen. "This is the best day of my life, son! I have been the (8) _____ for my company ever since I became the president, always getting blamed for everything that goes wrong. I didn't realize I had any (9) _____ to working there, but you made me see other possibilities. Now I realize what I've wanted to do all along — run a bowling alley! I don't care if I'm (10) _____ from the Millionaire Club. I'm opening a bowling alley, just like it said in the *Daily Scoop*.

Elton was stunned. He was happy. He was still Elton, though. "I want my own bowling ball and some new bowling shoes," he said. "And an unlimited supply of pizza . . ."

"Sure, son," smiled his father. "Sure. Whatever you want."

Super Challenge

Directions: Use the bonus words from the test to finish the story above.

Vocabulary List #2

whimsical: playfully odd or unusual

- The children's play features a **whimsical** tango by a frog and a swan.
- The Ballroom Blender Museum is popular for its **whimsical** sculptures of dancing food.

inadequate: not good enough; doesn't meet the requirements

- Jacob wasn't allowed to join the hockey team because his parents said his grades were **inadequate**.
- "That trout is **inadequate** to feed both of us," Russell said to Larry, who wasn't listening because he was happy just to have the first catch of the day.

contemplate: to look at or think about something carefully and thoughtfully

- Greta likes to sit in her backyard in the evening and **contemplate** life.
- The professor asked if anyone had ever **contemplated** the long-term effects of using a microwave oven.

humdrum: without change or variety; ordinary; dull

- Armand was bored with his **humdrum** life as an accountant, so he quit his job and became a race car driver.
- Many people take vacations to relieve the **humdrum** pace of everyday life.

vindicate: to clear of accusation or blame

- Accused of stealing frozen macaroni from the cafeteria, Debra was **vindicated** when two pans of it were discovered in the principal's office.
- Ella was **vindicated** when Bart confessed to painting the poodles green.

euphemism: a pleasant expression substituted for an unpleasant one

- Instead of "war," the king used the **euphemism** "conflict" in his announcement.
- Marty used a **euphemism** when she said she "borrowed" the coat. In fact, she stole it.

inhabited: lived in; occupied

- A tuba player **inhabited** the apartment next to the one for rent, so Rosa decided not to move in.

- Nobody likes a house **inhabited** by cockroaches, rats, ants, or Komodo dragons.

turf: someone's territory

- When his friends from the city came to visit him on the farm, Dan said with a grin, "You're on my **turf**, now."

- An argument over **turf** began when the girl in the Mickey Mouse costume and the guy dressed up like Goofy both wanted to be the first to greet visitors at the entrance to Disneyland.

colleague: a fellow member of a profession

- The professor had doubts about his **colleague's** invention, which had something to do with computer chips, doughnuts, blinking lights and peroxide.

- Many professionals ask their **colleagues** at the office for advice about problems.

stagnant: standing still; without movement

- The **stagnant** pool of water near the garage smelled terrible.

- Paul felt **stagnant** in his job at the restaurant; he knew he would always be a line cook and never the head chef.

Bonus Words

★scenario: an outline or summary of a chain of events

- "What happened? Here's what I see as the **scenario**," said the policeman at the crime scene.

- "I don't want to hear everything," said the play producer to the writer. "Just give me a **scenario**, and I'll let you know if I'm interested in reading the whole thing."

★nonchalant: casual; unconcerned

- Jared's mother was upset that he was so **nonchalant** about his bad report card.

- Even though her heart was pounding and her palms were sweaty, Misty tried to look as **nonchalant** as she could when she passed the bus full of football players.

Name _____

Test

Matching

Match each word in the left column to its correct definition in the right column.

_____ 1. humdrum

_____ 2. turf

_____ 3. whimsical

_____ 4. colleague

_____ 5. inadequate

_____ 6. vindicate

_____ 7. stagnant

_____ 8. euphemism

_____ 9. inhabited

_____ 10. contemplate

★Bonus words

_____ 11. scenario

_____ 12. nonchalant

a. playfully odd or unusual

b. standing still; without movement

c. an institution of higher learning

d. a pleasant expression substituted for an unpleasant one

e. lived in; occupied

f. an outline or summary of a chain of events

g. an unusual musical instrument

h. to look at or think about something carefully and thoughtfully

i. someone's territory

j. full of bad habits

k. to clear of accusation or blame

l. a fellow member of a profession

m. without change or variety; ordinary; dull

n. casual; unconcerned

o. not good enough; doesn't meet the requirements

p. to giggle

q. to wiggle

Fill-in-the-Blank

Directions: The first 10 words listed above belong in the story below. Read the story and use the clues in the text to place each word in the correct blank space provided. You may change the form of a word to fit the story, if you need to. (For example, you might need to add *ed*, *ing*, *ly* or *s*.)

Big Trouble

Jenny Starr was sick and tired of the way things were around her town. Everything always had the same (1) _____ feeling to it. Everything seemed to whisper to her, "Boorrrriiinngg!"

Her parents refused to listen to Jenny's complaints. They just couldn't understand why she couldn't find anything to do, especially since they themselves had so much fun, spending most of their time with their (2) _____ at the Broken Club Golf Course. Jenny gave up trying to convince them that nobody interesting (3) _____ their town.

One day, when Jenny was sitting in her yard, (4) _____ how she might find some entertainment, she saw a strange boy walking very quickly down her street. He was dressed in a/an (5) _____ costume of orange feathers and purple stripes. She began following him, repeating, "hey!" until he finally stopped and turned around.

"What do you want!" the boy said.

"No need to get upset," said Jenny. "I was just wondering why you're wearing that unusual costume."

"I'm on my way to (6) _____ myself. I have been falsely accused."

"Of what?" Jenny asked.

"None of your business," the boy said.

"Fine," said Jenny. "By the way, I was using a/an (7) _____ when I said 'unusual' costume. It's *weird*. Who are you, anyway?"

"I'm a superhero, and this is my territory."

"A superhero? Well, if you think this is your territory, you're mistaken. This is my (8) _____ and that's my sidewalk you're standing on."

"This is the territory I protect, and if it weren't for me, you'd be in big trouble by now," the boy said, crossing his arms. "Do you smell the water in that (9) _____ pond over there? It is filled with dangerous mutant creatures from another planet. They would crawl out every night and gnaw on your elbows, if it weren't for my Paralyzer Eye Beam."

"What kind of creatures?" Jenny asked suspiciously. "And what's a Paralyzer Eye Beam?"

"I only share that information on a need-to-know basis — and you don't need to know."

Jenny said, "I am not impressed. If you are a superhero, I think you are a pretty (10) _____ one. I'll take my chances with the mutant creatures."

"Suit yourself," shrugged the boy. He snapped his fingers, and a huge, lizard-like animal with seventeen eyeballs and long, purple claws emerged from the pond. Jenny screamed.

"Now you need to know," said the boy. "And it might be a good time to ask for help from my Paralyzer Eye Beam."

Super Challenge

Directions: Use the bonus words from the test to finish the story above.

Vocabulary List #3

devastate: to cause a lot of destruction or pain; to destroy

- Lily was **devastated** when her grandmother passed away.

- The hurricane **devastated** the island's poorest neighborhoods.

instinct: a natural behavior or sense that doesn't have to be learned

- As the speeding motorcycle rushed past her, Lynn's **instinct** was to cover her ears with her hands.

- Some pets know just by **instinct** when their owners need extra comforting after a bad day at work.

vintage: classic; of excellent quality and from a past era

- Rebecca has an entire closet full of **vintage** dresses.

- Ever since he bought his first 1936 Ford, Jerry had always wanted to open a **vintage** car dealership.

haggard: looking exhausted

- The old woman looked terribly **haggard** as she trudged along the street dragging her shopping cart.

- Gary's struggles with years of emphysema caused him to look **haggard** before his time.

pervasive: spreading out all over

- In the office, enthusiasm for Larry's new project was **pervasive**.

- The set for the new horror movie had a sense of evil about it that was **pervasive**.

suffrage: the right to vote

- Jane was angry when she read about the long struggle for women's **suffrage** in the United States and found that women could not vote here until 1920.

- The young man addressing the crowd believed that **suffrage** should be granted to all people in his country, not just the wealthy.

condescending: talking down to someone; acting superior to another person

- The students complained because the new student council president was **condescending**, acting as if she were better than everyone else.

- The bank president was **condescending** when he said to the business owner, "Now you understand that loans must be paid back, don't you?"

status quo: the way things are right now

- I don't want to change the mission of the company; I like the **status quo**.

- "Maintaining the **status quo** is not very challenging," the energetic new principal told his faculty on the first day of school.

reverberate: to echo again and again

- When the fire alarm malfunctioned, its noise **reverberated** throughout the hall for the rest of the day.

- On Christmas morning, church bells **reverberated** throughout the neighborhood.

drone: a low, deep, monotonous sound or hum that goes on and on

- George couldn't stand the **drone** he heard when his sister's band left the amplifier on.

- Ginny hated the **drone** of the auctioneer's voice over the loudspeaker.

Bonus Words

★flamboyant: showy; flashy

- Dara, a rather shy, quiet child, was tired of being compared to her **flamboyant** cousin, Sabrina.

- When she was running for class president, Doris decided to perk up her wardrobe with **flamboyant** hats that would attract a lot of attention.

★context: what leads up to and follows a statement and helps show its meaning

- In many tabloid newspapers, statements made by famous people are often taken out of **context** and distort the truth.

- He knew he would be misunderstood because they took his statement out of **context**, making it sound as if he disliked children.

Test

Matching

Match each word in the left column to its correct definition in the right column.

_____   1.   suffrage

_____   2.   reverberate

_____   3.   devastate

_____   4.   condescending

_____   5.   instinct

_____   6.   drone

_____   7.   vintage

_____   8.   status quo

_____   9.   haggard

_____   10.   pervasive

★Bonus words

_____   11.   flamboyant

_____   12.   context

a.   to echo again and again

b.   talking down to someone; acting superior to another person

c.   the feeling of raindrops falling on your head

d.   what leads up to and follows a statement and helps show its meaning

e.   the way things are right now

f.   an exact copy of something else

g.   spreading out all over

h.   a low, deep, monotonous sound or hum that goes on and on

i.   a natural behavior or sense that doesn't have to be learned

j.   the right to vote

k.   showy; flashy

l.   another name for a popular band of male singers

m.   looking exhausted

n.   to cause a lot of destruction or pain; to destroy

o.   classic; of excellent quality and from a past era

Fill-in-the-Blank

Directions: The first 10 words listed above belong in the story below. Read the story and use the clues in the text to place each word in the correct blank space provided. You may change the form of a word to fit the story, if you need to. (For example, you might need to add *ed, ing, ly* or *s.*)

What's All the Buzz About?

Cowboy Fred built his ranch many years before the new power plant came to town. For years, he was content to live by the light of lanterns. He had no use for a television, a dishwasher, or other electric appliances. All of his furniture was (1) _____ and he liked to live his life in an old-fashioned way.

Fred and his neighbors hadn't wanted a new power plant. However, when they showed up to vote, it turned out they didn't have (2) _____ in that district. The district had been redrawn so that only those living in the city could vote. The people in the city wanted the plant, so it was built.

The first problem came when the company turned on the main switch. Something malfunctioned, and there was a horrible clanging noise, which (3) _____ throughout the valley. After that, things settled down, but Fred heard a constant, low (4) _____ that drove him crazy. The hum was (5) _____ and he couldn't escape it. Soon, Fred started to look (6) _____ from his lack of sleep.

Fred's lack of sleep started to affect his work. He neglected his morning duties. He started missing cattle drives and forgetting to feed his horses. Fred went to the power plant manager and told him about the problem, but the manager just acted (7) _____ and talked to him as if he were a child.

Then Fred's neighbors decided to help. They called an emergency meeting in Fred's barn.

"People, the noise that comes from that stupid power plant is keeping Fred awake at night. He's our friend and a good rancher, too. What are we going to do?" Bill asked the crowd.

"What if Fred just moves?" Hank volunteered.

"Why should Fred have to move? He was here first!" Sue interrupted.

"Yeah! Right on!" everyone shouted.

"Quiet everyone!" said Bill. I know Fred's lack of sleep is affecting his work. If something doesn't change, this could (8) _____ his ranching business. He needs help. He's our friend, and we have to stand up for him."

"Bill's right," Lila said, "and I think we can challenge the (9) _____. Things can't just stay the way they are. But maybe Fred doesn't have to move, either. My (10) _____ tells me that there may be something we can do to change this situation. Here's my idea: Let's get all the people within the power plant area to shut off their electricity and go back to kerosene. That will get the power company's attention!"

"Yes," they all shouted, waking up Fred, who had been leaning against the wall, asleep. He was dreaming of all sorts of new, shiny, electric appliances.

Super Challenge

Directions: Use the bonus words from the test to finish the story above.

Vocabulary List #4

eloquent: smooth and persuasive in speech or writing

- Jeff's article about how students should get to pick more of their own classes was so **eloquent** that the principal was actually considering the idea.

- Keith admired his father's **eloquent** acceptance speech when he received the "Physician of the Year" award.

inevitable: unavoidable; certainly going to happen

- When Sharla got caught spray painting the wall, she knew that harsh punishment was **inevitable**.

- Little Richie is so bratty that it's **inevitable** that he will have a different baby sitter every time his parents go out.

guru: a person considered to be a guide or leader because of his or her magnetic personality

- Ghandi, who devoted his life to changing India's unfair governmental practices through peaceful resistance, is considered to be one of the most important political **gurus** of all time.

- Eleanor Lively's fans considered her the **guru** of telemarketing.

demure: pretending to be shy or modest

- Little Tammy was **demure** when her baby sitter first arrived, but as soon as her parents left, she became a wild child.

- For the funeral, Kendra put away her red leather mini skirt and looked **demure** in a navy blue ruffled dress with a high neckline and a mid-calf length skirt.

smolder: to burn with little smoke and no flame; to be angry but try to conceal it

- After the flames burned out, the garage continued to **smolder**.

- Dad's temper began to **smolder** as he listened to the man's ridiculous explanation for ramming the ice cream truck into his new Porsche.

stodgy: dull and stuffy

- Louis said the insurance seminar was full of **stodgy** salesmen who didn't appreciate his talent for making balloon animals.

- The **stodgy** college professor refused to approve the new course, "The Musical History of Bob Dylan."

indelible: permanent; unable to be removed or erased

- Lauren was sobbing because there was an **indelible** spot of green ink on her wedding gown.

- Owen would always remember his bicycle accident; it was **indelible** in his mind.

deterrent: obstacle; something that discourages something else from happening

- Bobby opposes the death penalty because he does not believe it is a **deterrent** to crime.

- The gate in front of the stairway was definitely a **deterrent** to the baby, who loved to crawl up the steps.

imply: to suggest without actually saying

- "Are you trying to **imply** that my kitchen is messy?" Jeff asked his mom when she handed him a mop and bucket.

- "When I offered you a stick of gum, I didn't mean to **imply** that you had bad breath. I just thought you might like some gum," Miranda explained to Leo.

apprehensive: nervous or uneasy; worried

- David couldn't sleep because he was **apprehensive** about the algebra test he didn't study for.

- Bill was **apprehensive** about meeting his blind date. "What if she's missing all her teeth and has green hair?" he thought.

Bonus Words

★rendezvous: a place where people have agreed to meet

- Mary and Susan agreed to a **rendezvous** at the Snack Shop after their bicycle rides around the park.

- The shelter on the north side of the mountain was their planned **rendezvous** for the night.

★plethora: a great amount of something

- After the little boy spilled grape jelly all over the kitchen counter, Annabelle discovered a **plethora** of ants in her pantry.

- The **plethora** of yelping poodles at the dog show drove Aunt Edie crazy.

Name _____

Test

Matching

Match each word in the left column to its correct definition in the right column.

_____ 1. indelible

_____ 2. stodgy

_____ 3. deterrent

_____ 4. imply

_____ 5. smolder

_____ 6. guru

_____ 7. inevitable

_____ 8. demure

_____ 9. eloquent

_____ 10. apprehensive

★Bonus words

_____ 11. plethora

_____ 12. rendezvous

a. a place where people have agreed to meet

b. nervous or uneasy; worried

c. pretending to be shy or modest

d. obstacle; something that discourages something else from happening

e. dull and stuffy

f. smooth and persuasive in speech or writing

g. a rare breed of goat

h. permanent; unable to be removed or erased

i. slightly more advanced in age

j. a person considered to be a guide or leader because of his or her magnetic personality

k. to burn with little smoke and no flame; to be angry but try to conceal it

l. a soap used to wash clothes

m. to suggest without actually saying

n. a great amount of something

o. unavoidable; certainly going to happen

Fill-in-the-Blank

Directions: The first 10 words listed above belong in the story below. Read the story and use the clues in the text to place each word in the correct blank space provided. You may change the form of a word to fit the story, if you need to. (For example, you might need to add *ed*, *ing*, *ly* or *s*.)

No Cure for Clowning Around

Clovis and Clem were twins who lived together in a small apartment in New Jersey. Everyone knew them as the Clown Twins. It was easy to tell them apart, though, because Clem always acted (1) _____, while Clovis was the outspoken one.

Other clowns in the city admired the Clown Twins and considered them to be (2) _____ in the field of clownery. The neighbors, however, were rather (3) _____ and hated living next to two guys who dressed up every day in fuzzy orange wigs, big red noses, purple and green striped overalls and huge floppy shoes.

Every morning, Clovis stood outside the apartment and gave a loud and (4) _____ speech about the greatness of being a clown. People stared at him as they walked by, but Clovis didn't care. He was proud to be a clown.

Clovis had a pet pig named Tulip. He loved Tulip with all his heart. He took her for walks every day. One day while he was walking Tulip, he saw a man smoking a cigarette. Clovis started to become a little (5) _____ because he knew that Tulip was afraid of smoke. When he saw the man walk in the other direction, though, he relaxed. He didn't notice that the man had tossed the cigarette into a pile of leaves.

As Clovis and Tulip approached the pile of leaves, Clovis saw that it was (6) _____. Tulip saw the smoke and started snorting, wiggling, and straining at her leash. Suddenly the leash snapped and Tulip ran in the opposite direction. Clovis followed her, but pigs can run very, very fast. He couldn't catch her. In a panic, he raced home and told Clem what had happened.

"Well, you know how much Tulip hates smoke," Clem said.

"Are you (7) _____ that it's my fault Tulip ran away?" said Clovis.

"No, not at all. I was just . . . ," Clem trailed off.

"Oh, you're right," wailed Clovis. "It's all my fault. When I saw the man with the cigarette, I should have turned around and gone in the other direction. I should have known that it was (8) _____ Tulip would take off if she got anywhere close to smoke."

Clovis was heartbroken. He stopped wearing his clown suit. He lost his sense of humor. He decided that the man with the cigarette was really the one to blame for the loss of Tulip. "There ought to be a/an (9) _____ to smoking in public places," he said. "Maybe people could get together and agree to yell at smokers." Then he thought of how much his neighbors hated his clown suit. "Or maybe we could make a law that required anyone smoking in public to wear a clown suit. Smokers would hate that!"

Animal control officers eventually found Tulip. After all, a pig in the city is pretty noticeable, and soon people were calling the animal control office with pig sightings. Clovis got his pig back, but the incident remained (10) _____ in his mind. With his brother Clem, he soon founded the Let's Embarrass Smokers Club of America.

Super Challenge

Directions: Use the bonus words from the test to finish the story above.

	1	2	3	4	5	6	7	8
V	suffrage	whimsical	eloquent	scapegoat	drone	punctilious*	stagnant	devastate
O	apprehensive	quotidian*	alternative	parody	irreverent	reverberate	indelible	contemplate
C	gala	condescending	context	inevitable	lollygag*	vintage	exposé	deterrent
A	smolder	affable	inhabited	flummox*	stodgy	scenario	humdrum	plethora
B	euphemism	haggard	rodomontade*	inadequate	rendezvous	colleague	oyez*	pervasive
R	flamboyant	ostracize	ashen	imply	status quo	guru	turf	flapdoodle*
A	ocellus*	nonchalant	instinct	demure	vindicate	barter	utopia	behemoth

Vocabulary List #5

spar: to argue or fight; to practice boxing

- Roberto liked to sneak into the gym late at night to watch his brother **spar** with the other boxers.

- "You really don't want to **spar** with me," warned the powerful senator, "because I'll win."

insinuate: to imply; to suggest or hint at indirectly

- "Are you trying to **insinuate** that my precious baby bulldog is ugly?" Lydia asked.

- When supermodel Sylvia Smyth started to put on a few pounds, her agent suggested that jogging might be a good idea, **insinuating** that she was getting too heavy.

modest: not conceited; limited in size

- The Duke of Dinkeydom was anything but **modest**, driving around in his stretch limo with the built-in hot tub.

- "It's hard to be **modest** when you've been elected prom queen two years in a row," Mia remarked.

precarious: uncertain; insecure; risky

- Little Max had a **precarious** hold on the edge of the fish tank when his mom found and rescued him.

- Russell's career as a stockbroker was **precarious** because he could never predict what was going to happen.

disclose: to reveal; uncover; make known

- The judge asked Six-Finger Louie to **disclose** the hiding place of the 12 karat diamond that he had stolen from the jewelry store.

- "If you finish my term paper for me, I won't **disclose** the fact that you sneaked out of the house last week to meet your boyfriend," Judith told her sister.

extravagant: wastefully expensive; excessive

- Myrtle thought that spending $75 on a pair of sandals for her two-year-old grandson was a little **extravagant**.

- When their 30th wedding anniversary was near, Mike decided to give Marge a really **extravagant** gift — a vacation to Hawaii.

bustling: busy; energetic and lively

- The toddlers at the preschool were a **bustling** group that exhausted the teacher.

- At 97, Gramma Haluska and her daughters, aged 74 and 76, were a **bustling** trio who never slowed down while they cooked Thanksgiving dinner.

smoke screen: any action used to try to cover up something

- When his parents found the broken taillight on their car, the sneaky teenager created a **smoke screen** by pretending to be extremely shocked.

- Some politicians create a variety of **smoke screens** to hide their past mistakes.

enlighten: educate; inform

- "I think I'd better **enlighten** you on the high cost of rent before you plan to move out of the house," said Mrs. Stenson to her eighteen-year-old son.

- Mr. Morgan felt the need to stop people on the street and **enlighten** them about the importance of wearing a helmet when riding a motorcycle.

transformation: a big change

- When his class started tenth grade, everyone noticed Jake's **transformation** from a short, chubby kid into a tall, lanky young man.

- The caterpillar goes through an amazing **transformation** when it turns into a butterfly.

Bonus Words

★fabricate: make up; invent

- Jonah's classmates were pretty sure he **fabricated** the part of the story about his family's escape from Iceland.

- The mad scientist was **fabricating** a quick and easy way for every Earthling to take weekend trips to the moon.

★debonair: gracious and charming, especially in social situations

- Marcos looked quite **debonair** as he strolled down the stairway in his tuxedo.

- Some older men look clumsy with their walking canes, but Sue's **debonair** grandfather swings his around gracefully.

Name _____

Test

Matching

Match each word in the left column to its correct definition in the right column.

_____ 1. insinuate
_____ 2. disclose
_____ 3. modest
_____ 4. smoke screen
_____ 5. bustling
_____ 6. spar
_____ 7. extravagant
_____ 8. precarious
_____ 9. transformation
_____ 10. enlighten

★Bonus words

_____ 11. debonair
_____ 12. fabricate

a. uncertain; insecure; risky
b. not conceited; limited in size
c. a big change
d. a kind of thistle
e. cloth used to make cloaks for royalty
f. gracious and charming, especially in social situations
g. make up; invent
h. to make a room brighter by turning on a lamp
i. to argue or fight; to practice boxing
j. to imply; to suggest or hint at indirectly
k. educate; inform
l. to reveal; uncover; make known
m. any action used to try to cover up something
n. busy; energetic and lively
o. wastefully expensive; excessive
p. type of netting used to keep cigarette butts from falling on sidewalks
q. humorous
r. humility

Fill-in-the-Blank

Directions: The first 10 words listed above belong in the story below. Read the story and use the clues in the text to place each word in the correct blank space provided. You may change the form of a word to fit the story, if you need to. (For example, you might need to add *ed, ing, ly* or *s.*)

Fine Home Furnishings

One day, as seventy-year-old Gretchen was walking to the market, she noticed a/an
(1) _____ group of people in front of a new store. She hurried toward the small crowd and saw her friend, Olga, trying to hold a large box that was (2) _____ balanced on her shoulder.

"Gretchen, it's a good thing you came down here when you did!" said Olga. The new furniture store just opened! You have to go inside! It wouldn't hurt you to spend some of your savings, you know," Olga said.

"Are you (3) _____ that I need more furniture?" Gretchen asked.

"No, not at all. I'm telling you *straight out* that you need more furniture!" Olga said.

"Remember what happened the last time a stranger opened a shop here? People ordered things, but the guy split town before they were delivered. When we found him, he put up a/an (4) _____ by pretending he was hard of hearing," Gretchen said. "I don't think anyone ought to buy things from this new guy."

"This is different!" Olga said. "Just wait until you see him!"

Gretchen decided to have a look. She pushed her way between two men who were angrily (5) _____ over the last remaining oak entertainment center and stepped inside.

The store was beautiful. A/An (6) _____ chandelier hung in the center of the room, gold with little crystals dangling from its arms. As Gretchen was staring at it, the owner approached her. She then turned to stare at him. He was a handsome man.

"Hello," he said. "Would you like me to (7) _____ you about the wonderful world of fine home furnishings?"

Gretchen nodded, still in awe over both the giant chandelier and the owner.

"I don't (8) _____ this to everyone because no one would believe me," the salesman said, "but my furniture is handmade by elves from Monrovia."

Gretchen's common sense deserted her. By the time she left the store, she had bought enough furniture to completely fill every room of her little house. She also had a date with the handsome owner. After she left the store, Gretchen had tea with Olga while the furniture was being delivered.

When Gretchen arrived home, the outside of her home looked exactly the same as it had for 50 years. But when she opened her front door, she was almost knocked over by the (9) _____ that had taken place. She smiled. Then she went to get ready for her big date. "I don't believe in Monrovian elves," she thought, "but I do believe I've met a man with good taste — in furniture and women." She blushed. "I guess I'm not being very (10) _____," she thought. Then she shrugged and laughed. "So what?"

Super Challenge

Directions: Use the bonus words from the test to finish the story above.

Vocabulary List #6

compulsory: required

- Even though she hated history, Alyssa signed up for the class because it was **compulsory**.

- Some politicians think that a high school education should be **compulsory**, but a lot of dropouts, obviously, do not.

biased: leaning toward one opinion over another for personal reasons; slanted or distorted

- Harry's mom swears he is the best fiddler in the world, but she is probably **biased**.

- The judge was **biased** against Betty because it was at his house that she threw the eggs.

radical: favoring extreme change

- "Your plan is way too **radical** for me," said Ed. "Can't you start with some smaller changes first?"

- Jamie is the **radical** one in her family. She thinks everyone should move to the mountains and eat only wild plants and berries.

persistent: refusing to give up; stubborn

- "That saleswoman is **persistent**," Cassie complained. "I finally bought that bad-smelling perfume just so she would leave me alone."

- Freddie was **persistent**. He asked Patty out fourteen times before he finally gave up.

inept: incompetent; not up to the task; bumbling

- When the waiter brought Katrina three burritos instead of the two cheeseburgers she ordered, she complained that he was **inept**.

- Jordan was so **inept** in the kitchen, that he was barely able to boil a pot of water.

surrogate: a substitute or stand-in

- Since Gabe's real grandpa lives far away, he thinks of his neighbor Mr. Cody as a **surrogate** grandfather.

- Mr. Cavella acted as a **surrogate** for the manager while she was home with the flu.

credentials: items or documents proving a person's identity or qualifications

- Quinn refused to let the police officer into her house until he showed proper **credentials**, like his badge.

- The doctor displayed his **credentials** on the wall of his lobby so people would know he was not a fraud.

disdain: scorn; contempt; an attitude that something is unworthy or not good enough

- Clyde is a devoted MacIntosh user and holds all PCs in **disdain**.

- "I have nothing but **disdain** for people who bet on greyhound races," declared the animal rights activist.

deluge: a floodlike rush of anything

- When the clothing store held its big buy-one-get-five-free sale, its employees faced a **deluge** of customers.

- The secretary nearly went crazy trying to answer the **deluge** of phone calls.

immune: protected against something harmful

- Sam must have been **immune** to the illness because everyone got sick except him.

- No matter how mean and nasty the other kids were to her, Gayle was not bothered. She was **immune** to their remarks.

Bonus Words

★**ostentatious:** showy, splashy; overly grand

- No matter what the weather, Fifi always wears a fur coat in an **ostentatious** display of her wealth.

- Snooty Mr. Clark has the most **ostentatious** house in the neighborhood.

★**faux pas:** the breaking of a social rule without necessarily meaning to

- Stephanie committed a **faux pas** when she first came to live with her host family and called the elderly grandmother by her first name.

- Carlos recognized his **faux pas** when the rest of the group members stared at him and then began inching away.

Name _____

Test

Matching

Match each word in the left column to its correct definition in the right column.

_____   1.   surrogate

_____   2.   radical

_____   3.   inept

_____   4.   compulsory

_____   5.   disdain

_____   6.   biased

_____   7.   deluge

_____   8.   immune

_____   9.   credentials

_____ 10.   persistent

★Bonus words

_____ 11.   faux pas

_____ 12.   ostentatious

a.   showy; splashy; overly grand

b.   putting on an ugly sweater

c.   refusing to give up; stubborn

d.   a floodlike rush of anything

e.   required

f.   a winter olympics event involving racing sleds

g.   scorn; contempt; an attitude that something is unworthy or not good enough

h.   incompetent; not up to the task; bumbling

i.   items or documents proving a person's identity or qualifications

j.   a substitute or stand-in

k.   favoring extreme change

l.   favoring chocolate over vanilla

m.   the breaking of a social rule without necessarily meaning to

n.   leaning toward one opinion over another for personal reasons; slanted or distorted

o.   protected against something harmful

Fill-in-the-Blank

Directions: The first 10 words listed above belong in the story below. Read the story and use the clues in the text to place each word in the correct blank space provided. You may change the form of a word to fit the story, if you need to. (For example, you might need to add *ed*, *ing*, *ly* or *s*.)

Computer Crisis

Mayor Gonzales knew it would be a long week when he checked his e-mail Monday morning and discovered his computer had a virus. He was furious. Why couldn't people just throw out their computers and do things on paper, the way they used to? He knew this was a/an
(1) _____ idea that no one would ever go for, but he liked it anyway.

At first he thought he might have done something incorrectly, but the
(2) _____ of phone calls that poured in a few minutes later confirmed his suspicion of a virus. Every city worker in town was having computer problems. It seemed that not a single computer in the county was (3) _____ to the virus. It affected them all.

Between the 31st and 32nd phone call, the mayor tried to talk with the county computer department. The line was busy. He tried again. It was still busy. "Hasn't anyone heard of 'redial waiting'?" he wondered. The mayor was (4) _____ though, pressing redial again and again until finally someone answered.

"This is the mayor," he said in his most authoritative voice. "This computer problem needs to be solved immediately."

"We're going to need outside help," said the head of the department.

"Well, tell whoever you get to bring a copy of his (5) _____. I don't want some (6) _____ fly-by-night swindler who has never even used a computer in his life coming in here and making things worse."

The mayor hung up and prepared to do some work on his laptop, which hadn't caught the virus and could serve as a/an (7) _____ for his other computer until it was fixed.

The phone rang. "Hey there, Mr. Mayor Man."

The mayor sighed. It was Maxwell Tweety. "Listen, Maxwell. I know you're upset about losing the race for mayor, but I'm very busy. I don't have time to deal with you right now." The mayor tried to be polite to his former opponent, but he just couldn't hide the (8) _____ he felt for Maxwell. From the beginning of the race to the end, Maxwell had pulled every dirty trick in the book, and the mayor didn't like him one bit.

Suddenly the mayor knew who was responsible for the vicious virus that was ravaging every computer in town. "Maxwell, you did this, didn't you? You sent the computer virus."

"What are you accusing *me* for, Mr. Mayor?"

"Well, you aren't good at anything else, but you are a genius with computers," said Mayor Gonzales.

"Are you (9) _____ against geniuses or something?" Tweety couldn't resist one last dig. "If *I* had been elected like I should have been, I would have made virus-detecting software (10) _____ for every computer in town. What kind of mayor are you, anyway?"

"A frustrated one," said Mayor Gonzales. What he was thinking, though, was something much, much worse.

Super Challenge

Directions: Use the bonus words from the test to finish the story above.

Vocabulary List #7

decisive: firm; clear; unmistakable

- Adele won the student council election by a **decisive** margin.

- The school principal gives no second chances. She takes **decisive** action against all students who break the rules.

apathetic: uninterested; lacking in strong feeling

- The teacher sighed at the **apathetic** students who were yawning, doodling on their notepads and staring out the window.

- The voters were so **apathetic** about the candidates that only 10 percent of them voted in the election.

manipulate: to manage or control shrewdly or unfairly; to act a certain way to get others to behave in ways that are beneficial to you

- Dori can **manipulate** almost anyone. All she has to do is cry and she usually gets what she wants.

- By picking and choosing which facts he presented, the speaker was able to **manipulate** the audience members into agreeing with him.

exempt: excused; not subject to the rules

- Mrs. Ramsey didn't have to pay taxes on the paper plates because the church she was buying them for was **exempt** from paying taxes.

- Just because Priscilla is the principal's daughter doesn't mean she is **exempt** from the rules.

revoke: to take back

- Boyd's parents **revoked** his driving privileges when he ran their car into a telephone pole.

- When the teacher found out Gordon cheated on the exam, she **revoked** the "A" she had given him.

defer: to postpone or delay

- The president had to **defer** the scheduled meeting because of a family emergency.

- Luke and Holly **deferred** the announcement of their engagement until Holly's father returned from his business trip.

literally: really; actually; word for word

- "When I said 'Go jump in a lake,' I didn't mean it **literally**," Kyla said to her little brother, who was soaking wet.

- When Kelly said the grass was greener on the other side, she meant it **literally**. On this side, the grass was brown and dying.

capacity: volume; the amount of space that can be filled

- Because the room soon filled to **capacity**, some people had to be turned away.

- Since Ms. Thurman's class was at **capacity**, the new student had to be assigned to Mr. Hanson's class.

fundamental: basic

- One of the **fundamental** rules of this school is that you respect other people.

- Gabriella didn't want any really hard classes, so she took "**Fundamentals** of Basket Weaving" instead of "Acid Solutions and Organic Chemical Compounds."

psychosomatic: having to do with physical symptoms caused by a person's thoughts or emotions

- John's illness was diagnosed as a **psychosomatic** response to the stress of losing his job.

- Melissa's nervousness about first dates always gave her a **psychosomatic** fit of vomiting right before her dates picked her up.

Bonus Words

★semblance: outward appearance

- The principal had a hard time regaining some **semblance** of order after the demonstrators left the auditorium.

- There wasn't even a **semblance** of understanding on the faces of the puzzled students as the teacher went on and on about participial phrases.

★hierarchy: a group arranged in order of rank from highest in power to lowest in power

- In the **hierarchy** of the feudal system, noblemen ranked higher than serfs.

- High school seniors usually receive more privileges than freshmen because they are at the top of the student **hierarchy**.

Name _____

Test

Matching

Match each word in the left column to its correct definition in the right column.

_____ 1. manipulate

_____ 2. apathetic

_____ 3. decisive

_____ 4. defer

_____ 5. revoke

_____ 6. exempt

_____ 7. literally

_____ 8. capacity

_____ 9. psychosomatic

_____ 10. fundamental

★Bonus words

_____ 11. hierarchy

_____ 12. semblance

a. to take back

b. to take on a date

c. basic

d. excused; not subject to the rules

e. a group arranged in order of rank from highest in power to lowest in power

f. firm; clear; unmistakable

g. to manage or control shrewdly or unfairly; to act a certain way to get others to behave in ways that are beneficial to you

h. volume; the amount of space that can be filled

i. dude

j. dud

k. to postpone or delay

l. having to do with physical symptoms caused by a person's thoughts or emotions

m. really; actually; word for word

n. uninterested; lacking in strong feeling

o. outward appearance

Fill-in-the-Blank

Directions: The first 10 words listed above belong in the story below. Read the story and use the clues in the text to place each word in the correct blank space provided. You may change the form of a word to fit the story, if you need to. (For example, you might need to add *ed, ing, ly* or *s*.)

Ms. Lingle's True Calling

Ms. Lingle was a school librarian. However, what she really wanted to do was start a traveling polka band and tour the islands of the Caribbean.

It wasn't that Ms. Lingle didn't love books. She did. In fact, she read them all the time. However, she was tired of students checking out books and never returning them by the due date. Did they think they were (1) _____ from the rules or something? Even if they finally did turn in their books, they always wanted to (2) _____ payment of their fines.

Ms. Lingle wanted to take (3) _____ action against the perpetrators. She wanted to (4) _____ the library privileges of anyone who had books overdue by even one day. Unfortunately, Principal Findlay wouldn't let her, reminding her that books, even if they were overdue, were good for kids. "Learning," he explained, "is the (5) _____ purpose of school, and students learn a lot from books." Knowing the principal was right, but having no other solution herself, Ms. Lingle grew (6) _____ about her job. Instead of making changes to improve the library, she sat on her stool behind the check-out counter day after day, dreaming of sand, sun and cute little cabanas cleverly shaped like pineapples.

After three weeks of daydreaming, the miserable Ms. Lingle became quite ill. Seeing immediately that the illness was (7) _____, probably caused by her unhappiness with her job, Ms. Lingle's doctor advised her to make a change in her life.

"All right, Ms. Lingle, here's my prescription: Reach for the stars." Staring straight ahead, the miserable Ms. Lingle slowly raised her arms in the air. The doctor laughed.

"No, Ms. Lingle, I didn't mean for you to take my words (8) _____. What I mean is, do something you've always wanted to do."

Ms. Lingle's eyes brightened. Immediately she thought of her polka band and a straw-covered Caribbean nightclub filled to (9) _____. There would be standing room only. She would be a star!

Three weeks later a postcard arrived for Principal Findlay. Filling in as the school librarian had left him almost too exhausted to read his mail. The students, through tears, pleading, and promising, had (10) _____ him into letting them check out 25 books each and keeping them as long as they wished. The library shelves were empty, and Principal Findlay didn't know what to do.

With a defeated sigh, he leaned over the check-out counter, read the delightful account of Ms. Lingle's opening night in Barbados, and grabbed a piece of stationery.

"Dear Ms. Lingle . . ." he began. "Please come back. Pretty please come back. Pretty, pretty please with a cherry on top come back."

Super Challenge

Directions: Use the bonus words from the test to finish the story above.

Vocabulary List #8

legendary: well-known; famous

- Almost every U.S. school child knows about Paul Revere's **legendary** ride through the night.

- Smitty's delicious cinnamon rolls were **legendary** throughout the countryside.

scrutinize: to look at or examine closely

- The doctor **scrutinized** the X-rays for half an hour before she finally found a tiny crack in the bone.

- Kelly **scrutinized** her term paper before turning it in. She didn't want it to have any errors.

nomad: a wanderer who has no fixed home

- Roy was a **nomad**, wandering from city to city in search of a job.

- In their retirement, Arlen's grandparents have become **nomads**, driving all over North America in their RV.

caricature: a cartoon-like picture of someone, with exaggerated features

- An artist drew a **caricature** that made Mr. Beeman look like a duck.

- If you think you have a big nose in real life, you should see what it would look like in a **caricature**.

parched: dry and thirsty

- The worst thing about living in the middle of the desert is that you're always **parched**.

- After playing tennis in 104-degree heat, Nina was so **parched** that she drank three bottles of Gatorade.

defiant: openly and boldly resisting or challenging

- When Mr. Gulley asked Ursula to open her book, she **defiantly** threw it on the floor.

- Chloe is so **defiant** that others are embarrassed to be around her when she talks to her parents.

clad: dressed; clothed

- When Harold started to leave for school **clad** in shorts and a T-shirt, his grandma yelled, "Are you crazy? It's 30 degrees outside!"

- The handsome knight was **clad** in sparkling armor.

subtle: not obvious; only hinted at

- You can't always be **subtle** with Shannon. If you want her to do something, you have to spell it out.

- The taste of basil in the spaghetti sauce was so **subtle** I hardly knew it was there.

spontaneous: acting on impulse instead of planning it out

- Wade likes to plan out his evenings, but Jada likes to be more **spontaneous**.

- When Bert **spontaneously** took a plane to New York one afternoon, no one could believe it.

improbable: not likely

- Niko hadn't studied at all, so his parents thought it **improbable** that he would pass his driver's test.

- Since her mom hated cats and her dad hated dogs, it was **improbable** that Melanie would ever have a pet.

Bonus Words

★quash: to put an end to

- "We need to **quash** that rumor immediately!" cried the alarmed school board member.

- The government **quashed** the rebellion before it became violent.

★atrophy: to shrink or waste away

- If you spend a month in a wheelchair, the muscles in your legs might **atrophy** and make it difficult to walk when you get out.

- "Don't let your brains **atrophy** from disuse over the summer," the teacher warned his students on the last day of school.

Name _____

Test

Matching

Match each word in the left column to its correct definition in the right column.

_____ 1. caricature

_____ 2. clad

_____ 3. defiant

_____ 4. nomad

_____ 5. legendary

_____ 6. spontaneous

_____ 7. parched

_____ 8. improbable

_____ 9. subtle

_____ 10. scrutinize

★Bonus words

_____ 11. atrophy

_____ 12. quash

a. to shrink or waste away

b. not likely

c. acting on impulse instead of planning it out

d. to put an end to

e. dressed; clothed

f. not dressed

g. well-known; famous

h. to look at or examine closely

i. a wanderer who has no fixed home

j. a type of writing paper

k. something you get when you win a race

l. openly and boldly resisting or challenging

m. dry and thirsty

n. a cartoon-like picture of someone, with exaggerated features

o. not obvious; only hinted at

p. a method of cooking an egg

Fill-in-the-Blank

Directions: The first 10 words listed above belong in the story below. Read the story and use the clues in the text to place each word in the correct blank space provided. You may change the form of a word to fit the story, if you need to. (For example, you might need to add *ed*, *ing*, *ly* or *s*.)

Sick of Social Studies

Ethan was sick of social studies. He didn't want to learn about the (1) _____ King Tut, no matter how famous he was. And he didn't want to hear about all those (2) _____ of the Sahara desert. What was so great about them, anyway? All they did was wander around in the sun, (3) _____ in long flowing robes. That must have been so hot. Those people were probably always (4) _____.

Speaking of being thirsty, Ethan was absolutely dying of thirst. Then his teacher asked a question. (5) _____, Ethan raised his hand. Then he realized he had no idea what he was doing. Why did he raise his hand? And now the teacher probably expected him to have some kind of answer to some question. What nerve!

Ethan looked around at his classmates, hoping for some (6) _____ clue about what the question might have been. The teacher looked at him expectantly. Finally, he came up with an answer. "Uh . . . George Washington. It was George Washington who was the father of our country. And he was the father of Egypt, too. He built all those pyramids himself."

Ethan's teacher looked at him like he was from another planet. "I think that's highly (7) _____, Ethan, since George Washington never came within a hundred miles of Africa. And since he was born several centuries after the pyramids were built." Then he (8) _____ Ethan's face. "Are you feeling all right?" he asked. "Do you need to go see the nurse?"

"Or maybe a psychiatrist," said Amy Wanner.

Ethan was angry and embarrassed. "I don't need to go see anybody!" he shouted (9) _____.

"Maybe you ought to try paying attention," said his teacher mildly and then continued his lecture about the pyramids.

Ethan consoled himself by drawing a/an (10) _____ of his teacher — and it was not very flattering. He added a powdered, George Washington-style wig and then threw a pyramid into the background. And then at the last minute he drew Amy Wanner's face off to the side — with the body of a camel.

Super Challenge

Directions: Use the bonus words from the test to finish the story above.

	1	2	3	4	5	6	7	8
V	manipulate	improbable	fabricate	defiant	scombroid*	insinuate	revoke	radical
O	deluge	malarkey*	faux pas	surrogate	decisive	punka*	nomad	transformation
C	hierarchy	disclose	palaver*	clad	debonair	exempt	bustling	ostentatious
A	malapropism*	apathetic	compulsory	spar	credentials	smoke screen	caricature	quash
B	subtle	inept	scrutinize	paronomasia*	biased	precarious	capacity	parched
R	extravagant	quidnunc*	immune	semblance	enlighten	defer	disdain	fundamental
A	legendary	persistent	literally	clerihew*	spontaneous	psychosomatic	atrophy	modest

Vocabulary List #9

supplement: to add something, especially to make up for something lacking

- Miss Kingston decided to **supplement** her teaching income by working evenings at the library.
- Joe was still hungry after lunch, so he **supplemented** his three bologna sandwiches with a bowl of soup.

collate: to gather and put in order

- The secretary **collated** the 12 pages of the report just in time for the meeting.
- It's a good thing Victor stapled all pages he had **collated** before his sister turned on the fan.

nestle: to settle down comfortably and snugly

- The children were **nestled** in their beds — except for Harry, who was downstairs watching TV.
- Cheryl didn't like going out in the cold, so she used the snowy day as an excuse to **nestle** into her old beanbag chair and read a mystery.

unintelligible: cannot be understood

- Jessica woke up after her surgery, muttered something **unintelligible** and went back to sleep.
- "I never know what my baby sister wants," Greg complained. "All her sounds are **unintelligible** to me."

imminent: likely to happen right away

- The fortune teller warned Sheila to skip her flight to Florida because a plane crash was **imminent**.
- Cory didn't want to call his mom at work and confess spilling chocolate milk all over the computer because he knew that a long lecture would be **imminent**.

painstaking: very careful; taking great pains

- Constructing a castle out of toothpicks is **painstaking** work.
- Cindy's **painstaking** efforts to glue every little window onto the tiny model car gave her a headache.

reprehensible: deserving severe criticism

- Darren's behavior was so **reprehensible** that even his best friends no longer wanted anything to do with him.

- "I don't care how good-looking Walter is," Tanya said. "I would never go out with him after the **reprehensible** way he treated his last girlfriend."

gaudy: tastelessly showy

- Brendon preferred the quiet countryside over Las Vegas, which he thought was rather **gaudy**.

- Lindsay's diamond, ruby and sapphire ring was so **gaudy** that everyone made fun of it behind her back.

sporadic: happening only from time to time, with no pattern or order

- Tyler's **sporadic** efforts to improve his grades weren't enough to make a difference.

- Although she would like to be more disciplined about keeping her diary, Evelyn makes only **sporadic** attempts to write regularly.

surpass: to go beyond; exceed

- Ronald was sure his recipe for Chocolate Sugary Delight Pie would **surpass** all the other recipes and win him first prize in the bake-off.

- Chad **surpassed** all his competitors and won the track meet's highest medal.

Bonus Words

★complacent: self-satisfied and content

- Regina was **complacent** about the upcoming beauty pageant and didn't feel she needed to practice her talent number.

- Since Alex was **complacent** about his "C+" grade point average, he didn't bother to do any extra credit.

★bona fide: genuine

- "This is a **bona fide** 18th century bed pan," Penelope bragged.

- When the expert told Megan the huge gem she found in the cave was a **bona fide** diamond, she jumped up and down shouting "I'm rich! I'm rich!"

Name _____

Test

Matching

Match each word in the left column to its correct definition in the right column.

_____	1.	imminent
_____	2.	sporadic
_____	3.	nestle
_____	4.	supplement
_____	5.	unintelligible
_____	6.	collate
_____	7.	painstaking
_____	8.	reprehensible
_____	9.	gaudy
_____	10.	surpass

a. tastelessly showy
b. deserving severe criticism
c. genuine
d. very careful; taking great pains
e. to add something, especially to make up for something lacking
f. cannot be understood
g. a place where birds live
h. to go beyond; exceed
i. self-satisfied and content
j. an instrument used on ships to determine true north
k. to settle down comfortably and snugly
l. happening only from time to time, with no pattern or order
m. deserving praise
n. to gather and put in order
o. likely to happen right away

★Bonus words

_____	11.	complacent
_____	12.	bona fide

Fill-in-the-Blank

Directions: The first 10 words listed above belong in the story below. Read the story and use the clues in the text to place each word in the correct blank space provided. You may change the form of a word to fit the story, if you need to. (For example, you might need to add *ed*, *ing*, *ly* or *s*.)

Blizzard on Basketball Day

Although the bus was freezing and they had to be covered in blankets, the Pillsboro High School girls' basketball team members felt lucky to be (1) _____ in their seats and on their way to the state championships. It had snowed (2) _____ all day long, with icy rain coming down between each snowfall. The girls had been afraid the principal would call off the trip and make them forfeit the game, an idea every one of the players thought was (3) _____. They would not have forgiven him!

The girls need not have worried. The principal was busy with the school's brand new state-of-the-art copy machine and its state-of-the-art stacking and organizing feature, which
(4) _____ the copies instead of making the busy principal perform the
(5) _____ task himself. He didn't care one bit that many of the teachers thought the new copy machine, with its hot pink lights, rhinestone-studded door and gold-plated buttons, was kind of (6) _____ . This copy machine (7) _____ all others when it came to efficiency. It was going to save him oodles of time.

When the day of the state championships rolled in with a snow storm at its heels, the principal was too busy reading the 1200-page copy machine booklet to notice. The blizzard flaring up periodically outside his office window drew no attention at all from him. He was too busy saving oodles of time.

Back on the bus, the coach was slumped in a seat at the front, exhausted from working nights at the Coffee Cabana to (8) _____ her measly teaching income. Growing a little concerned about the bad weather, Liza, the team's first-string forward, made her way down the aisle to tell the coach about the blizzard. The coach, however, only muttered something (9) _____ and went back to sleep.

Luckily, the bus eventually made it to the state championships. Slogging their way into the gym through the drifting snow, Liza and the rest of the girls felt very lucky. They knew that a win for their team was (10) _____ . If a blizzard couldn't keep them down, nothing could.

Super Challenge

Directions: Use the bonus words from the test to finish the story above.

Vocabulary List #10

deteriorate: to get worse

- Because she was afraid her husband's condition would **deteriorate** before the ambulance could arrive, Mrs. Pablo took him to the hospital herself.

- The cabin had **deteriorated** so much in 12 years that Charles didn't even recognize it.

immense: very large

- Karl was lost in an **immense** forest and he didn't think he would ever find his way out.

- Your back yard might seem small to you, but to a ladybug, it is **immense**.

solemn: serious or formal

- Mrs. Henderson believed that children should be taught to behave at **solemn** occasions like funerals.

- The judge looked very **solemn** as he addressed the court.

urban: having to do with the city

- If you like subways, tall buildings and lots of people, you would probably enjoy living in an **urban** area.

- Jake and Laura decided not to get married since he wanted to live on a farm two hours from the nearest store and she wanted to live somewhere more **urban**.

vague: not clear or precise

- Since the teacher's instructions for the test were so **vague**, the students in the class had no idea what they were supposed to do.

- Because the description of the bank robber was so **vague,** the police didn't think they would ever find him.

rural: having to do with the country, not the city

- Devony lives in a **rural** part of Colorado where she sees wildlife every day and bright stars every night.

- Walter lives in a **rural** area of only 500 people.

frail: physically weak or delicate

- Theodore was afraid to pick up his 17-year-old cat since she was so thin and **frail**.

- Jessica looks **frail**, but she's actually so strong that she has run in two marathons.

juvenile: a child or young person

- Since the movie was rated "R," **juveniles** couldn't see it unless they were with their parents.

- Vivian works with **juveniles** in trouble with the law, hoping to help them so that they don't end up becoming part of the adult prison population.

trivial: unimportant

- Polly thought her teacher's rules were rather **trivial**. That's why she had to stay after school so often for detention.

- "I know you may think this is **trivial**," Bart said, "but I just want to point out that you got 25 pieces of popcorn and I only got 23."

wither: to dry up or decay

- Beverly forgot to water her roses and they quickly began to **wither**.

- Dawn hates winter because everything that was beautiful in the summer has **withered**.

Bonus Words

★indigo: a deep violet or blue color

- The twins have very different taste in blue jeans. Mikayla likes hers to be a faded, very light blue. Heidi likes hers to be a deep **indigo**.

- Sometimes the sky at night is blue, and sometimes it is black. But sometimes it's a really pretty shade of **indigo**.

★vibrant: lively; sparkling; radiant

- Mary's **vibrant** smile lights up a room.

- As soon as the Spears moved into their new home, they painted over the boring beige walls with a more **vibrant** lemon color.

Name _____

Test

Matching

Match each word in the left column to its correct definition in the right column.

_____ 1. wither

_____ 2. trivial

_____ 3. rural

_____ 4. immense

_____ 5. vague

_____ 6. frail

_____ 7. juvenile

_____ 8. deteriorate

_____ 9. solemn

_____ 10. urban

★Bonus words

_____ 11. indigo

_____ 12. vibrant

a. serious or formal

b. to dry up or decay

c. a type of head covering

d. having to do with the country, not the city

e. lively; sparkling; radiant

f. to get worse

g. a popular board game

h. very large

i. an incurable disease

j. a child or young person

k. not clear or precise

l. a deep violet or blue color

m. physically weak or delicate

n. unimportant

o. having to do with the city

p. quiver

q. liver

Fill-in-the-Blank

Directions: The first 10 words listed above belong in the story below. Read the story and use the clues in the text to place each word in the correct blank space provided. You may change the form of a word to fit the story, if you need to. (For example, you might need to add *ed, ing, ly* or *s.*)

Zinnia's Grandmother Plants an Idea

Zinnia was always bringing her grandmother old (1) _____ plants to nurse back to health. Grandma Flora had become (2) _____ over the years, but she was still strong enough to work with plants. In fact, she had such a way with them that she could make even the most dried up geranium healthy again.

On Tuesday, when Zinnia went to her grandmother's room, Mr. Hawthorne was there. He and Zinnia's grandmother were comparing the differences in how they grew up. Zinnia's grandmother had been a small-town girl, born and raised in (3) _____ Kentucky

with her nearest neighbors two miles away. Mr. Hawthorne had grown up in a/an
(4) _____ environment — Los Angeles, California. "My memories are a little
(5) _____," he apologized, "but it seems to me that even in those days the cars
were packed on the roads tighter than sardines in a can. Smelled about as good, too," he
added, laughing as he tapped his cane. "And I think with all the pollution around, the condition of air quality in most cities has (6) _____. It's worse now than it was then,
yet many people still view pollution as a/an (7) _____ problem. They are wrong!
It's a/an (8) _____ problem!"

  Soon he was talking about *everything* that was worse today than in the good old days.
"Nobody reads anymore," he complained, with a/an (9) _____ look on his face.
"Nobody knows how to make a good peach pie from scratch. Nobody knows how to save
money. Nobody knows how to darn socks or iron a shirt so that it looks good. And kids
today?" He shook his head. "They have no respect for their elders. Why, when I was a/an
(10) _____, young people were supposed to be seen and not heard. They knew
their manners. They knew how to dress right, too. Girls wore *skirts*, not pants. Boys wore
decent slacks, not these baggy pants hanging down and . . ."

  Zinnia's grandmother interrupted. "Zinnia, I just had a thought. Why don't you run to the
store for me and get some milk? When you come back, Mr. Hawthorne and I will be finished
visiting, and you and I will share some cookies I have saved just for you." She winked at
Zinnia. She knew that Mr. Hawthorne could get carried away.

  Zinnia smiled as she left. "Grandma Flora knows as much about kids as she does about
plants," she thought approvingly as she walked outside.

Super Challenge

Directions: Use the bonus words from the test to finish the story above.

Vocabulary List #11

meander: to wander aimlessly

- Liz likes to walk straight to class, but Bethany likes to **meander**.

- Instead of sticking to geology, Ms. Fritch usually **meanders** onto other subjects like surfing and the Beatles concert she went to twenty-five years ago.

lavish: extravagant; more than enough

- Instead of crackers and cheese, Daisy put out a **lavish** spread that included caviar, shrimp, imported cheeses and truffles.

- Richard wanted a simple wedding in his mother's flower garden, but Fifi wanted a **lavish** celebration at the Ritz.

nausea: a feeling of being sick to the stomach, including the impulse to vomit

- Whenever Kim sets foot on a boat, she has feelings of **nausea** and has to run to the bathroom.

- The **nausea** Harry felt when he sniffed the sour milk was obvious from the shade of green he turned.

fraud: a person who is not what he or she pretends to be; a fake or a phony

- Janie thought the telemarketer was a **fraud**, so she didn't donate to the charity he was supposedly representing.

- Everyone discovered that the Santa Claus was a **fraud** when little Freddie McIntyre yanked his beard off.

petty: unimportant; trivial

- Paula and Sandy decided it was silly to end their friendship over something as **petty** as whose turn it was to drive.

- Toby's **petty** complaints about his socks not matching his underwear were driving his mother crazy.

accumulate: to pile up, gather or collect

- Drew liked to **accumulate** comic books so much that there was hardly room left in his bedroom for his bed.

- Jerry wrote his girlfriend's name in the dust that had **accumulated** on his trombone.

buffoon: someone who is always clowning around

- It is nearly impossible to have a serious conversation with Adam when he is behaving like such a **buffoon**.

- Cora is such a **buffoon** that it was no surprise at all when she won the leading role in the drama club comedy.

zany: extremely silly or foolish

- Tara's uncle loves the **zany** humor of Jim Carey.

- Quincy is way too serious to pull a stunt as **zany** as super-gluing thirty pairs of old tennis shoes to the gym floor.

puny: small or weak

- After he watched the Superman movie, Terry's little brother toddled around flexing his **puny** biceps.

- Ned was **puny** until the 9th grade. Then he quickly grew to be the biggest player on his high school football team.

colossal: huge

- Cleaning up after the massive flood was a **colossal** task for the Stevens family.
- Jordan knew it was a **colossal** mistake to tell the principal to go suck an egg.

Bonus Words

★vaudeville: a type of variety show popular before radio and television, consisting of short acts such as juggling, comic skits, songs and dance routines, etc.

- They laughed and laughed at the **vaudeville** show, especially when the juggling comedian performed.

- Since they all had a variety of talents, the girls decided to do an old-fashioned **vaudeville** show for their fundraiser.

★mayhem: intentional violence or destruction

- The pictures of **mayhem** sent back from the battlefield sickened the war pro-testers.

- The substitute teacher was fired when the principal saw the **mayhem** he was allowing in the classroom.

Name _____

Test

Matching

Match each word in the left column to its correct definition in the right column.

_____ 1. meander

_____ 2. accumulate

_____ 3. petty

_____ 4. zany

_____ 5. buffoon

_____ 6. colossal

_____ 7. puny

_____ 8. lavish

_____ 9. nausea

_____ 10. fraud

★**Bonus words**

_____ 11. vaudeville

_____ 12. mayhem

a. a person who is not what he or she pretends to be; a fake or a phony

b. small or weak

c. extremely silly or foolish

d. the sound you make when you clear your throat

e. "fatal error; illegal operation" message

f. huge

g. a feeling of being sick to the stomach, including the impulse to vomit

h. unimportant; trivial

i. to wander aimlessly

j. to pile up, gather or collect

k. extravagant; more than enough

l. intentional violence or destruction

m. a small town in Vermont

n. someone who is always clowning around

o. a type of variety show popular before radio and television, consisting of short acts such as juggling, comic skits, songs and dance routines, etc.

Fill-in-the-Blank

Directions: The first 10 words listed above belong in the story below. Read the story and use the clues in the text to place each word in the correct blank space provided. You may change the form of a word to fit the story, if you need to. (For example, you might need to add *ed*, *ing*, *ly* or *s*.)

The Corndog Caper

Herbert and Doug thought it would be a clever prank. The plan was to saw off the (1) _____ plastic corn dog from the top of Kernal Korncob's Korndog Shack and drag it over to the football field.

"We need you to be the lookout," Doug begged his sister Linda, who knew this was just another one of Herbert's (2) _____ ideas. Herbert was always planning adventures like jumping a box car and riding to the next town to stay in a/an (3) _____ hotel he could never afford, or entering a weight-lifting contest even though he was so

(4) _____ he could barely lift his own backpack. But when it came time to actually go on the adventure, Herbert would say he was grounded and couldn't make it. Linda thought Herbert was just a/an (5) _____, always pretending to be brave when he wasn't.

"How are you going to get the corn dog off the roof?" asked Linda.

"Oh, we'll figure it out," said Doug. "We're not worried about a/an (6) _____ detail like that."

Linda sighed, but she agreed to be the lookout for this latest scheme. Why? It was one more thing she could use against Herbert. She hoped to (7) _____ so much evidence against him that she could convince her brother to ditch him as a friend and start hanging around with the popular, cool guys at school. That way, she figured, they would come to their house to see her brother and wind up noticing her and asking her out. All she had to do was get Herbert out of the picture.

Herbert, Doug and Linda planned to meet at the Korndog Shack at midnight on Sunday. Linda was sure Herbert wouldn't show up, so she (8) _____ around the block, imagining how happy she would be when her brother gave up on Herbert. Imagine how surprised she was to look up and see Herbert dragging a ladder down the street. As he propped it against the building, Linda said, "Hey! You're here."

"Of course I'm here," said Herbert. Somehow, he had sensed that he *had* to show up this time.

Doug held the ladder and Herbert started climbing. Then he made the mistake of looking down at the ground far below him. A feeling of (9) _____ came over him. How could he have forgotten that heights made him sick to his stomach? He looked down at Doug in dismay.

Then he threw up, all over Doug. Doug yelled and let go of the ladder, and Herbert came tumbling to the ground. "He's such a/an (10) _____," thought Linda, as she helped him up. He looked so pathetic she almost felt sorry for him.

Then she looked at her brother, who was frantically trying to find a garden hose. The person she really felt sorry for was him.

Super Challenge

Directions: Use the bonus words from the test to finish the story above.

Vocabulary List #12

voracious: unable to be satisfied

- Salvador decided to become a librarian because he was a **voracious** reader.

- Ellie had a **voracious** appetite. That's why her bill at Burger King was so huge.

reiterate: to repeat

- "I know I said this once before, but I want to **reiterate** that you are not to wear shorts to church tomorrow — even if it is 100 degrees," Dara's mother warned.

- To make sure Jerry understood her, Katie **reiterated** her answer: "No, no, and no. I do not want to go out with you. I do not."

begrudge: to be jealous of

- "My so-called friend Nina **begrudges** every good thing that happens to me," Cindy complained.

- Hank **begrudged** his sister the spelling bee trophy. "I know I spell better than her," he complained.

pacifist: someone who is opposed to violence for any reason

- Rachel would not enlist in the military because she was a **pacifist**.

- "If I weren't a **pacifist**, I would beat you up," Tony screamed at his older brother, who was teasing him.

omniscient: all-knowing

- "Roger raises his hand every time the teacher asks a question," Molly complained. "Does he think he's **omniscient** or something?"

- Dale thought he was so sneaky about stealing cookies that when his mother still managed to find out about it, he assumed she must be **omniscient**.

superfluous: unnecessary or irrelevant

- Ely explained to his mother that since he was already wearing a wool hat and sweater, his coat would only be **superfluous**.

- No wonder Garth didn't have any money for rent. His budget was full of **superfluous** expenses like hot air balloon rides and jewelry-making kits.

morose: gloomy

- Maggie is joyful and jolly. Mindy is **morose**; she's always frowning.
- Harvey hoped that moping around the house and looking **morose** would make his dad feel sorry for him and un-ground him.

permeate: to pass through or spread over something

- The meeting was dragging until Calvin got there. His happiness and good humor **permeated** the room.
- Everybody at the Halloween party knew that Ross was the ghost because the strong cologne he always wore **permeated** his sheet.

repertoire: all the numbers a performer is prepared to perform

- "Mary Had a Little Lamb" is only one of the songs in Susan's **repertoire** for the accordion recital.
- The Pickwick Theater has over thirty plays in its **repertoire**, including *Grease* and *The Music Man*, which it performed last fall.

animosity: extreme hatred

- The **animosity** Amber felt for Jared when he stood her up for the prom was extreme.
- With her mean personality and her big mouth, Marcie attracted a lot of **animosity**.

Bonus Words

★incognito: dressed to disguise your identity

- Not wanting to attract any attention, the movie star made her trips to the grocery store **incognito**.
- The terrorist left the country **incognito** and was never heard from again.

★chagrin: embarrassment or annoyance

- Martin was full of **chagrin** when his date told him that his fly had been down most of the afternoon.
- Mr. Frantella was **chagrined** to see pools of oil all over his new driveway.

Name _____

Test

Matching

Match each word in the left column to its correct definition in the right column.

_____ 1. begrudge

_____ 2. omniscient

_____ 3. repertoire

_____ 4. morose

_____ 5. voracious

_____ 6. animosity

_____ 7. superfluous

_____ 8. reiterate

_____ 9. permeate

_____ 10. pacifist

★**Bonus words**

_____ 11. chagrin

_____ 12. incognito

a. having a lively personality

b. to repeat

c. unnecessary or irrelevant

d. all the numbers a performer is prepared to perform

e. something you do to your hair to make it curly

f. to pass through or spread over something

g. dressed to disguise your identity

h. shining with an inner light

i. to be jealous of

j. someone who is opposed to violence for any reason

k. extreme hatred

l. unable to be satisfied

m. all-knowing

n. gloomy

o. embarrassment or annoyance

p. raven

q. nevermore

Fill-in-the-Blank

Directions: The first 10 words listed above belong in the story below. Read the story and use the clues in the text to place each word in the correct blank space provided. You may change the form of a word to fit the story, if you need to. (For example, you might need to add *ed*, *ing*, *ly* or *s*.)

Mario's Mix-up

Mario refused to join his family for dinner, opting instead to play one sad song after another on the piano in the living room. Since the piano music (1) _____ the thin walls of his family's apartment, everyone at the dinner table became almost as depressed as Mario himself.

"Can't you play something more cheerful?" his dad shouted between bites. "I'm getting so depressed I can hardly eat my dinner." Knowing what a/an (2) _____ appetite his dad had, especially for pork chops, Mario tried hard to play some of the happier songs in his (3) _____. But try as he might, the songs still sounded sad.

"I want to (4) _____, Mario, that I would like you to play something more cheerful. Your mother's crying over her food, and it's not because of the onions."

Mario tried again. But even "Happy Days Are Here Again" sounded sad when you were like poor Mario and mourning the loss of your girlfriend of three entire weeks. He wasn't just mourning her loss, though. He was (5) _____ her good fortune. In the week since he had broken up with her, Cynthia had made the soccer team, become vice-president of student council and won the state math competition. What was she planning next, an Olympic gold medal he wondered?

Mario was so upset he wanted to pound his head on the piano, but he had always been a/an (6) _____ and wasn't going to start beating up on anyone, especially himself. Instead, he just kept playing.

An hour later, after Mario's family had gone out for ice cream to cheer themselves up, the phone rang.

"Mario? This is Cynthia. Listen, I just saw your parents at Ice Cream Heaven. They said you were pretty down. I'm not pretending to be (7) _____ or anything, but I have a hunch this is because of our break-up. I just want you to know that I don't feel any (8) _____ toward you or anything for dumping me. Like you said, we can 'still be friends.' And besides, I have to get ready for the Olympic trials. I might make the soccer team, you know."

"What do the Olympic trials have to do with anything?" asked Mario.

"That information is (9) _____, and besides, *you* dumped *me*!"

"I did not!" Cynthia said.

"Then how is it that we're not together anymore?" Mario said.

"Beats me. I thought. . ."

"Wait a minute," Mario said, "I think we have a case of miscommunication here."

"Miscommunication? How about *no* communication! This is all Betsy's fault. She told me that you wanted to dump me."

"What!? She told me *you* wanted to dump *me*!"

"Well," Cynthia said, "I guess Betsy isn't my best friend anymore. That makes me mad, but it makes me sad, too. Do you think you could play one of your sad songs for me on the piano?"

Mario smiled. "Sure, Cynthia, I can do that. So, are we back together?"

"Yes," Cynthia said.

When Cynthia stopped by his house, Mario tried and tried to play a song that sounded (10) _____, but every piece just made Cynthia smile and smile and smile.

Super Challenge

Directions: Use the bonus words from the test to finish the story above.

	1	2	3	4	5	6	7	8
V	urban	salmagundi*	supplement	reiterate	manticore*	incognito	lavish	colossal
O	omniscient	accumulate	juvenile	puny	reprehensible	vague	begrudge	painstaking
C	wither	nestle	voracious	deteriorate	indigo	palooka*	mayhem	buffoon
A	oology*	permeate	gaudy	meander	frail	complacent	hallux*	vibrant
B	bona fide	solemn	fraud	albedo*	collate	immense	morose	surpass
R	imminent	animosity	quixotic*	chagrin	sporadic	repertoire	trivial	zany
A	petty	unintelligible	vaudeville	rural	pacifist	nausea	thrasonical*	superfluous

Vocabulary List #13

subsequent: coming after; following

- Ms. Arriaga warned Gilbert that any **subsequent** tardies would mean detention.
- After Jack failed his algebra test, he hired a tutor and did better on **subsequent** tests.

ambitious: determined; eager for power, wealth or success

- Paige was **ambitious** about making the Olympic team, so she practiced her swimming seven hours every day.
- Mr. Hart is an **ambitious** man who will stop at nothing to get what he wants.

bigot: a very prejudiced person

- "I don't want to go anywhere near that guy passing out racist literature," said Lou. "He's the worst **bigot** I've ever seen."
- "We can't have a **bigot** like that working here!" cried Mr. Spears. "We have to work with people of all ages and ethnic groups!"

enchanted: charmed or delighted

- "I'm **enchanted** with the idea of a costume party!" said Miss Dawson with a smile.
- Mr. Ashton was pleased to see how **enchanted** his daughter was with the ballet at the performing arts center.

essential: absolutely necessary

- If you don't have gills, then scuba gear is **essential** for breathing underwater.
- Aunt Lydia always said that a pound of butter is **essential** for a decent batch of oatmeal cookies.

sparse: few and far between; not dense or crowded

- Since clues at the scene of the crime were **sparse**, the detective knew she would have trouble solving the case.
- The population in Wyoming is **sparse**.

wager: to bet

- Donald decided to **wager** on getting the check in time to pay the bill.
- Margaret and Daisy **wagered** a chocolate shake on who would be first to get a date to the prom.

frugal: thrifty

- Instead of going with the expensive name-brand jeans, Haley was **frugal** and bought the lesser-known brand.
- Joe and Mick were **frugal** with their allowances because they were saving money to go to the big game at the stadium.

haggle: to bargain over something or argue in an attempt to come to terms

- Shelly loved to **haggle** over the price of things at garage sales.
- "Stop **haggling** over the details and just sign the contract," the salesman said.

demented: insane

- The **demented** professor drank the green, bubbling liquid in the beaker.
- Zoe thought her sister was **demented** to go out with a conceited and inconsiderate guy like Roger Simms.

Bonus Words

★gall: rude boldness

- Victor couldn't believe his sister had the **gall** to bring a hamburger to the vegetarian picnic.
- "How can you have the **gall** to ask me out again right after you stood me up?" cried Eleanor.

★callous: unfeeling; insensitive

- Laughing at an injured puppy is a pretty **callous** thing to do.
- "Maybe it's **callous**, but I really hope my sister doesn't get to play the role of Cinderella," Jody said.

Name _____

Test

Matching

Match each word in the left column to its correct definition in the right column.

_____ 1. essential

_____ 2. sparse

_____ 3. enchanted

_____ 4. bigot

_____ 5. wager

_____ 6. demented

_____ 7. frugal

_____ 8. subsequent

_____ 9. haggle

_____ 10. ambitious

a. determined; eager for power, wealth or success

b. to bargain over something or argue in an attempt to come to terms

c. coming after; following

d. the part of a faucet where the water comes out

e. rude boldness

f. thrifty

g. to bet

h. a mean woman

i. few and far between; not dense or crowded

j. absolutely necessary

k. unfeeling; insensitive

l. to repeat a phrase over and over in a religious ceremony

m. charmed or delighted

n. a very prejudiced person

o. insane

★Bonus words

_____ 11. callous

_____ 12. gall

Fill-in-the-Blank

Directions: The first 10 words listed above belong in the story below. Read the story and use the clues in the text to place each word in the correct blank space provided. You may change the form of a word to fit the story, if you need to. (For example, you might need to add *ed*, *ing*, *ly* or *s*.)

Jordan's Wish

Jordan couldn't decide what was the worst part about shopping with his mom at garage sales. It may have been her (1) _____ goals. Each Saturday she wanted to visit every single garage sale in a 20-mile radius and find the very best deals at each one. She became so focused that Jordan sometimes thought she might be slightly (2) _____. He even considered trying to get her to a psychiatrist because that crazed look she got every time she drove up to a sale gave him the creeps.

Maybe it was how (3) _____ she became when she stepped onto those lawns with all those tables full of junk. Suddenly, 10 cents was too much to pay for a teapot. A dollar was too much to pay for a chair. She (4) _____ over the prices until the sellers gave in, just to get rid of her.

One day, as they walked up yet another driveway full of tables, Jordan said, "Mom, I don't mean to be a/an (5) _____ or anything, but I think people at garage sales are kind of gross, and I don't want to have to be around them anymore. I'll finish the day with you, but I'm not going with you to any (6) _____ garage sales. This is the very last one."

Jordan was happy to have come clean with his mom, until he realized she wasn't listening to him at all. She was eyeing a table that looked (7) _____. It had only three items on it, and one of them was a strange looking vase.

"Oh, what a gorgeous vase! I absolutely have to have it," his mother said.

"Mom, do you really need another vase?" Jordan asked.

"Yes, it is (8) _____ that I have that vase in my living room. Jordan, how much do you want to bet I can get it for less than a quarter?"

Jordan was irritated that she hadn't listened to him. "Mom, I am not going to make a/an (9) _____ with you over how much money you'll pay for a stupid vase. That's dumb."

Before he could finish, his mother was on her way over to the person with the cash box. Jordan wandered over to see just what the big deal was with this vase. Then the strangest thing happened. When he picked up the vase, it shook and grew cold in his hand. The colors around the rim swirled and looked almost alive. Was this vase (10) _____? Did it have some kind of magical power? Suddenly a genie popped out in a cloud of smoke. Jordan looked around to see everyone's reaction, but nobody seemed to notice.

"Are you invisible?" Jordan asked.

"No, not exactly, but I only appear to people who are really, really bored."

"Well, that's me, all right," Jordan said, "at least until you showed up."

"You get three wishes, you know," the genie said.

"Yes, I know. My first wish is easy. Make my mom stop going to garage sales!"

Super Challenge

Directions: Use the bonus words from the test to finish the story above.

Vocabulary List #14

heathen: a person seen as uncivilized or not religious

- "Only **heathens** skip church on Sunday!" roared the minister to the congregation.

- Casey's grandmother says her neighbors are **heathens** because they are loud and they don't take baths or comb their hair.

enhance: to improve

- A lot of the pictures of models you see in the magazines have been **enhanced** to make the models look better than they really do.

- Justin was a good cook, but he wanted to **enhance** his skills, so he took a cooking class.

bungle: to mess up something because of clumsiness

- Harvey tried to sound smooth and sophisticated when he asked Brittany out, but he was so nervous he **bungled** the whole thing.

- The thieves **bungled** their break-in by stepping on the burglar alarm and setting it off.

lenient: mild in discipline and punishment

- Everyone thought the new teacher would be **lenient**, but she ended up being very strict.

- Michael's dad is pretty **lenient** about his son's behavior since he only sees him every other weekend.

anonymous: unidentified; unknown

- "We never print **anonymous** letters," said the newspaper editor.

- Tashawna gets a lot of **anonymous** notes from secret admirers.

zest: intense enjoyment

- Marilyn had such a **zest** for life that she never wanted to waste a minute of it watching television.

- Esteban sang his solo with such **zest** that no one even cared that he was off key.

sprawl: to spread out

- When Susan came home from work, her son and his friends were **sprawled** out on the floor playing Nintendo.
- Tammy's St. Bernard always **sprawls** in the doorways so no one can walk through.

sieve: a strainer

- Martha began to cry over her lumpy gravy. Her ex-husband had taken the **sieve** she always used to make it smooth and creamy.
- To get the larger rocks out of a handful of sand, run the sand through a **sieve**.

envious: jealous of someone for having something you want

- Shy little Madeleine was **envious** of how her sister Annie made friends so easily.
- Mark is **envious** of Brian's ability to throw the football so far.

nimble: able to move quickly and easily

- Jenny isn't as **nimble** as Jack. When she tried to jump over the candlestick, she fell flat on her face.
- Whenever the class played dodge ball in gym, Nancy won because she was so **nimble**.

Bonus Words

★cache: a safe place for hiding things

- "I've got a **cache** of Tootsie Rolls stashed in my dresser drawer," Yolanda bragged. "That way I don't have to go downstairs at all if I'm mad at my mom."
- The pirates hid a **cache** of jewels on the deserted island.

★repugnant: offensive; repulsive

- Alicia didn't care if her friends called her a chicken. The idea of lying to her parents was **repugnant**.
- The smell floating up from the sewer was **repugnant**.

Name _____

Test

Matching

Match each word in the left column to its correct definition in the right column.

_____ 1. heathen

_____ 2. nimble

_____ 3. envious

_____ 4. sprawl

_____ 5. zest

_____ 6. anonymous

_____ 7. lenient

_____ 8. enhance

_____ 9. sieve

_____ 10. bungle

a. mild in discipline and punishment
b. to improve
c. a new kind of thimble
d. intense enjoyment
e. to mess up something because of clumsiness
f. a strainer
g. having a tendency to lean on things
h. a brand of dish soap
i. unidentified; unknown
j. able to move quickly and easily
k. a safe place for hiding things
l. to spread out
m. a person seen as uncivilized or not religious
n. jealous of someone for having something you want
o. offensive; repulsive
p. showing great bravery

★Bonus words

_____ 11. repugnant

_____ 12. cache

Fill-in-the-Blank

Directions: The first 10 words listed above belong in the story below. Read the story and use the clues in the text to place each word in the correct blank space provided. You may change the form of a word to fit the story, if you need to. (For example, you might need to add *ed*, *ing*, *ly* or *s*.)

The Lesson

When Henry's mom opened his bedroom door on Saturday morning, he was
(1) _____ out on his double bed surrounded by colored pencils, drawing paper and comic books.

"What a mess! Now get out of that bed and get dressed for your piano lesson," she yelled.

All week long, his mom was pretty easy going and (2) _____ about his sloppy room and his tendency to draw cartoons instead of doing his homework. She hardly ever yelled at him. But when it came to those piano lessons, she was strict. He had to go, even if he wanted to quit.

Saturday mornings were torture for Henry. He was so (3) _____ of his sister. She got to sit around and watch TV instead of going to piano lessons. Plus, his piano teacher, Professor Bidenmider, didn't like him one bit. He called Henry "an idiot, a/an (4) _____, a disgrace to the human race" and sometimes worse, just because he wasn't so great at playing the piano. The professor constantly reminded him, "Put life into the music; play with some (5) _____!"

Today when Henry walked into the professor's house for his lesson, his heart flip-flopped in his chest. Jolene, the most gorgeous girl in his class, was sitting right there in the chair he usually sat in himself. Henry sneaked into the room, sat in the corner, turned his back and tried to remain (6) _____.

"Hey, Henry. Do you take lessons here, too? I usually come on Friday afternoon, but I couldn't make it yesterday. I was so glad — until my dad told me he set up a make-up lesson for me. I guess I'll have to go after you."

Henry nodded, and tried to think of some way to keep her from hearing Professor Bidenmider yell at him. Just then, Professor Bidenmider poked his head out of the door and pointed at Henry. It was time.

"Come on now, Henry," he said to himself. "Don't (7) _____ this. Play better than you ever have in your life."

Henry took a deep breath and started to play. To his surprise, he played beautifully. His fingers were (8) _____ as they went gracefully up and down the keyboard. He was inspired. He even added a little musical flourish at the end to (9) _____ the quality of the piece (and impress Jolene, of course). At the end, he looked up at the professor, pleased with himself. But the professor was frowning.

"You idiot," he shouted. "You have a mind like a/an (10) _____. I gave you wonderful advice last week and you just let it all fall through the holes in your brain. Play it again!"

When the horrible lesson was finally over, Henry flew out the door, vowing to tell his mom he refused to go to any more piano lessons. He tried to hurry past Jolene, who laughed as he passed her.

"I thought I was the only one he yelled at. I feel so much better," she said.

On the way home, Henry tried to figure out how to convince his mom that Friday afternoon was a much better time for a piano lesson.

Super Challenge

Directions: Use the bonus words from the test to finish the story above.

Vocabulary List #15

dormant: inactive

- Some seeds can lie **dormant** for years before they finally sprout.
- After being **dormant** for over 100 years, the volcano erupted.

nuptial: having to do with marriage or a wedding

- The bride and groom listened to a moving **nuptial** toast by the best man.
- The **nuptial** feast included smoked salmon, champagne, white cake and small mints shaped like bells.

fluctuate: to vary; to rise and fall

- The temperature tended to **fluctate** between 60 and 75 degrees.
- Trent's attitude toward school **fluctuated** greatly. Sometimes he wanted straight A's and sometimes he didn't care if he passed at all.

expletive: an exclamation that is obscene or profane

- Rhonda lost her job as student council president when she used an **expletive** over the intercom during morning announcements.
- Little Sally's mouth dropped open when she heard her neighbor kick the broken lawnmower and utter an **expletive**.

pompous: full of exaggerated self-importance

- The **pompous** prince insisted on having a footstool made of gold.
- The president was so **pompous** in dealing with his staff members that all of them despised him.

pilfer: to steal small amounts at a time

- The boss fired Ms. Coolidge because of her tendency to **pilfer** money from customer accounts.
- For years, Freddie **pilfered** pennies from his sister's piggy bank to buy red licorice.

indigent: poor

- Don felt sad when he saw an **indigent** family pushing a shopping cart down the street.

- The missionary was shocked at the number of **indigent** people who had to come to him for help.

commend: to praise

- "I **commend** you for trying," the piano teacher said to her student. "Now, if you could just get a few of the notes right," she thought to herself.

- Sidney was **commended** for her clean-up efforts after the big flood.

chic: stylish; fashionable

- Most of the movie stars wore long, **chic** gowns to the awards ceremony, but some of them looked really tacky.

- The young women at Hancock Jr. High School thought it was very **chic** to wear their clothes inside out. Their parents just thought it was ridiculous.

authoritarian: very strict; expecting total obedience

- Principal Bellar's **authoritarian** approach to running the school was turning both students and teachers against her.

- Abby couldn't help noticing the similarities between Mussolini's **authoritarian** government and Mr. Musso's history class.

Bonus Words

★comprehensive: extensive; broad; including all the details

- The book Frank chose to consult was the most **comprehensive** one he could find on the subject of reptiles in North America.

- Jeff's class notes were so **comprehensive** that even his teacher asked to borrow them from time to time.

★adroitly: skillfully; cleverly; expertly

- The candidate **adroitly** dodged the issue of his past whenever anyone asked him a tricky question.

- The quarterback **adroitly** avoided being sacked.

Name _____

Test

Matching

Match each word in the left column to its correct definition in the right column.

_____ 1. expletive

_____ 2. dormant

_____ 3. indigent

_____ 4. pilfer

_____ 5. pompous

_____ 6. authoritarian

_____ 7. chic

_____ 8. commend

_____ 9. fluctuate

_____ 10. nuptial

a. to vary; to rise and fall

b. a baby chicken

c. to steal small amounts at a time

d. to praise

e. a game similar to golf, but less exciting

f. having to do with marriage or a wedding

g. stylish; fashionable

h. full of exaggerated self-importance

i. poor

j. skillfully; cleverly; expertly

k. extensive; broad; including all the details

l. a type of cheerleading outfit

m. an exclamation that is obscene or profane

n. inactive

o. very strict; expecting total obedience

p. pineapple-flavored

★Bonus words

_____ 11. comprehensive

_____ 12. adroitly

Fill-in-the-Blank

Directions: The first 10 words listed above belong in the story below. Read the story and use the clues in the text to place each word in the correct blank space provided. You may change the form of a word to fit the story, if you need to. (For example, you might need to add *ed*, *ing*, *ly* or *s*.)

Harvey the Fashionable

Although he was right in the middle of the (1) _____ dinner following his daughter's wedding, the king could not get his mind off the last opinion polls taken by Sir Harvey, his most trusted aide.

"I just don't understand it, Harvey. Why do the people's opinions of me (2) _____ so greatly? It seems that one minute they (3) _____ me for a job well done, and the next minute they talk of overthrowing me."

"To be sure, Sire, I'm not at all sure," said Harvey, looking down at some cake crumbs on his purple satin overcoat, embroidered in real gold. He was the best-dressed person in the kingdom.

He was also the most (4) _____. He turned to a servant and said, "Tend to these crumbs, immediately. Get a brush and make sure my coat is spotless!!! I am the king's most trusted advisor! I should not have crumbs on my coat, ever!!!" With his nose in the air, he turned back to the king. "Perhaps you should change your style. Be more (5) _____. Carry a big stick. Show them who's boss. And, if I may suggest, Your Highness," said the nobleman with a sneer, "have the tailor make you something more (6) _____ to wear. Those knee-huggers went out with the last dragon-slaying."

"I think this problem is bigger than my clothes, Harvey. There are hundreds of (7) _____ families in the land, families that can't even afford a loaf of bread each week. I would gladly give them every gold coin I have, but I fear someone has (8) _____ so much money over the years that there is very little left in the treasury." Suddenly he took a close look at Harvey's clothes. Where had all the money for those elegant shirts, coats and knickers come from?

A quick investigation showed that Harvey was indeed responsible for the treasury's lack of money. The king was furious. His temper had been (9) _____ for twenty years, never once coming to the surface and showing itself. Now, however, he exploded. He yelled and yelled and yelled, terrifying everyone in the castle. He even uttered a/an (10) _____, shocking the queen so much that she fainted.

He also fired Harvey, auctioned off all of his clothes and gave the money to the poor. Harvey left the palace in disgrace, in search of a more fashion-conscious king to serve.

Super Challenge

Directions: Use the bonus words from the test to finish the story above.

Vocabulary List #16

preliminary: coming before the main part or main action; introductory

- Jason won the **preliminary** heat in the 100-yard dash and was preparing for the finals when he tripped and broke his leg.

- Since the **preliminary** hearings had taken so long, John's trial was delayed another month.

temperamental: easily upset; moody

- One of the kids Sara baby-sits is easy-going and predictable. The other is so **temperamental** Sara never knows whether he's going to smile or burst into tears.

- Logan is a skilled soccer player, but he often gets thrown out of the game because he is so **temperamental**.

pious: very religious

- A nun is probably more **pious** than most other people.

- Rudy is so **pious** that he goes to church each morning before work.

menacing: threatening

- Alec saw the **menacing** black clouds roll in about 10 minutes before the tornado struck the barn.

- The bully gave a **menacing** stare, and all the kids ran home.

bedraggled: wet, limp and dirty

- Since it had been caught out in a rainstorm, Stephanie's little kitten looked **bedraggled**.

- Polly looked **bedraggled** after the soccer match on the muddy field.

clamor: to cry out, demand or complain noisily

- Tyler was a quiet baby, but Tessa would constantly **clamor** for attention.

- The employees went on strike, **clamoring** for better working conditions.

jeopardy: danger or risk

- Rita put her scholarship to college in **jeopardy** when she got a "D" in chemistry.
- When the pirate took out a torch and lit it, the captain knew his ship and his crew were in **jeopardy**.

whim: a sudden desire or idea; a passing fancy

- "I just did it on a **whim**," Emma complained, looking at the huge roadrunner tattooed on her shoulder.
- On a **whim**, Butch decided to go skydiving and discovered that he loved it.

adjacent: next to

- Emily hated the new seating arrangement because she was **adjacent** to her former boyfriend, Frank Thigbee.
- The new coffeehouse is **adjacent** to the supermarket and across the street from the gas station.

synonymous: similar or identical in meaning

- "I don't want you hanging out with Mary Prink anymore," warned Emily's mother. "That girl's name is **synonymous** with *trouble*."
- The goals of the Nature Club are **synonymous** with the goals of the Environmental Crusaders.

Bonus Words

★formidable: causing fear, alarm or dread

- Writing a twenty-page report is a **formidable** task, but you can do it if you are organized.
- Natalie was such a **formidable** opponent that most of her competitors backed out of the race.

★nebulous: unclear; vague; indefinite

- The teacher's guidelines for the assignment were so **nebulous** that the students had no idea how to begin.
- Between the extremes of good and bad, there is a **nebulous** gray area.

Name _____

Test

Matching

Match each word in the left column to its correct definition in the right column.

_____ 1. adjacent

_____ 2. jeopardy

_____ 3. preliminary

_____ 4. synonymous

_____ 5. whim

_____ 6. menacing

_____ 7. temperamental

_____ 8. pious

_____ 9. bedraggled

_____ 10. clamor

a. similar or identical in meaning

b. coming before the main part or main action; introductory

c. easily upset; moody

d. very religious

e. unclear; vague; indefinite

f. a mass of interstellar gas

g. threatening

h. wet, limp and dirty

i. causing fear, alarm or dread

j. to cry out, demand or complain noisily

k. danger or risk

l. next to

m. underneath

n. to trip over something clumsily

o. a sudden desire or idea; a passing fancy

p. describes something moved by being pulled over the ground

★Bonus words

_____ 11. nebulous

_____ 12. formidable

Fill-in-the-Blank

Directions: The first 10 words listed above belong in the story below. Read the story and use the clues in the text to place each word in the correct blank space provided. You may change the form of a word to fit the story, if you need to. (For example, you might need to add *ed*, *ing*, *ly* or *s*.)

Running Out of Patience

Mrs. Harper had about had it with her daughter. First, Natalie brought home a/an (1) _____ puppy that tracked mud all over the house. Then, on a/an (2) _____, she put herself and her whole family in (3) _____ by seeing if a plastic bag would melt if she put it in a skillet and turned on the burner.

It did. In the process, she managed to catch her sleeve on fire. Her mother ran into the room, snatched up Natalie and threw her into a snowdrift that was (4) _____ to the house. Then, as her little brother Ned (5) _____ for attention, Natalie decided to bonk him on the head with the nutritious snack her mother had given her — a stalk of celery. Ned immediately started crying, of course.

"What did you do to him?" Mrs. Harper demanded.

"Oh, nothing," said Natalie. "He's so (6) _____. You just never know. One minute he's happy, and the next he's crying his head off."

Ned got a/an (7) _____ look on his face. He looked like he was about to bonk Natalie on the head with his Tonka truck. Mrs. Harper quickly grabbed the truck, though she did have at least a little sympathy for Ned's impulses.

As her mother was serving lunch, Natalie took one look at her plate and grimaced. Was that slimy green stuff what she thought it was? Was it spinach? As far as Natalie was concerned, spinach was (8) _____ with garbage. "I hate spinach," she whined. "I won't eat it."

Her mother glared at her. Natalie recognized that look. It was a look that was usually (9) _____ to more drastic action, like sending Natalie to her room. Natalie decided to act quickly. She got a/an (10) _____ look on her face and said sweetly, "I can't eat it. It's against my religion."

Natalie's mother glared harder. Natalie looked at her mother's face. Then she looked at the spinach. "Um . . . I think my religion says it's okay to eat spinach if I put salt on it." She grabbed the salt shaker and gave her mother what she hoped was an endearing smile.

Just then the stray puppy bounded in and bit into her mother's leg. As Mrs. Harper let out a yelp, Natalie decided it would be a very, very good idea to eat that spinach, no matter how bad it tasted.

Super Challenge

Directions: Use the bonus words from the test to finish the story above.

	1	2	3	4	5	6	7	8
V	nebulous	enchanted	bungle	clamor	indigent	haggle	menacing	nimble
O	burgomaster*	bedraggled	envious	grommet*	authoritarian	callous	expletive	bigot
C	fluctuate	heathen	flabbergast*	formidable	sparse	sprawl	pilfer	chic
A	sieve	incunabulum*	temperamental	zest	cache	jeopardy	katzenjammer*	adjacent
B	frugal	commend	subsequent	preliminary	nuptial	palimpsest*	comprehensive	demented
R	whim	gall	anonymous	essential	wager	synonymous	repugnant	pompous
A	ambitious	lenient	pious	dormant	mondegreen*	enhance	maelstrom*	adroitly

Vocabulary List #17

smattering: small amount

- When the principal said he wanted to lengthen the school year, he received only a **smattering** of applause.

- Lenore ruined the turkey, mashed potatoes and dressing before she admitted she had only a **smattering** of experience with cooking.

priority: something that ranks first in importance or urgency

- For Wanda, hitting all the best dance clubs took **priority** over studying, and that is why she flunked all her classes.

- Unless you make fitness a top **priority**, you probably won't find the time to exercise.

obliterate: to wipe out, destroy or erase

- Sue vowed to **obliterate** the competition for head cheerleader by performing six back handsprings and a straddle jump.

- Jay's compact car was **obliterated** in the accident. Luckily, all he had was a broken arm.

haughty: proud and vain to the point of being scornful of others

- The **haughty** president of the club refused to consider Flo for membership because of the way she dressed.

- Dr. Gable was so **haughty** in accepting his award that he offended most of the people in the audience.

degrading: humiliating; shameful

- After he wrecked his BMW, Sid found it **degrading** to have to drive his grandmother's 1982 Oldsmobile.

- Mark thought having to clean the bathrooms at school was **degrading**, and he complained to the school board about his punishment.

retort: a sharp, quick or witty reply or response

- "Whenever someone insults me," Louis complained, "I can't think of a good **retort** until much later."

- Robert insulted Marietta, but her **retort** had everyone laughing at Robert.

martyr: a person who chooses to suffer or die rather than give up his or her faith or beliefs

- Joan of Arc was a **martyr** who chose to die rather than give up her Christian faith.

- After his death, it was clear that the **martyr** had inspired the entire country with his courage and committment to the cause.

notorious: well-known for unfavorable reasons

- Ms. McCanless was **notorious** for giving the hardest tests in the school.

- Billy the Kid was a **notorious** outlaw from the Old West.

equivalent: equal in value, quantity, degree, etc.

- Jenny swore she had read somewhere that the fat in her favorite kind of hamburger was **equivalent** to a whole stick of butter.

- Bella swore that her pain was **equivalent** to the feeling of being in a vat of lemon juice with paper cuts all over her body.

lacerate: to tear or mangle

- "I'm afraid this blade could easily **lacerate** an employee's hand, " said the efficiency inspector, looking at the new machine.

- The mother shrieked when she saw her daughter's **lacerated** knee.

Bonus Words

★tainted: contaminated or corrupted

- Kate and Maggie were thrilled when their parents discovered their little brother's lie, and his goody-two-shoes image was **tainted**.

- "Oh no," the straight-A student sobbed. "This 'B' in science has **tainted** my perfect record!'"

★anachronism: something that is out of place in a historical sense

- "This movie is set in the Middle Ages, but that knight is wearing a digital watch!" laughed Julia. "That's certainly an **anachronism**."

- The CD player in Fred Flintstone's living room is definitely an **anachronism**.

Name _____

Test

Matching

Match each word in the left column to its correct definition in the right column.

_____ 1. priority

_____ 2. degrading

_____ 3. martyr

_____ 4. equivalent

_____ 5. notorious

_____ 6. retort

_____ 7. haughty

_____ 8. obliterate

_____ 9. smattering

_____ 10. lacerate

★Bonus words

_____ 11. tainted

_____ 12. anachronism

a. to smooth down rough gravel

b. contaminated or corrupted

c. to tear or mangle

d. something that is out of place in a historical sense

e. a bite-size pastry

f. small amount

g. humiliating; shameful

h. a person who chooses to suffer or die rather than give up his or her faith or beliefs

i. to wipe out, destroy or erase

j. proud and vain to the point of being scornful of others

k. the fear of spiders

l. equal in value, quantity, degree. etc.

m. a sharp, quick or witty reply or response

n. something that ranks first in importance or urgency

o. well-known for unfavorable reasons

p. stained a dark color

Fill-in-the-Blank

Directions: The first 10 words listed above belong in the story below. Read the story and use the clues in the text to place each word in the correct blank space provided. You may change the form of a word to fit the story, if you need to. (For example, you might need to add *ed, ing, ly* or *s*.)

The Fortunate Accident

Bernadette threw on her favorite shorts and was almost out the front door when her little sister Kat jumped in front of her and held onto the doorknob. Getting in Bernadette's way seemed to be Kat's highest (1) _____. She lived for it. "Where are you going?" she demanded.

"To your funeral, if you don't get out of the way." Bernadette felt bad about her mean (2) _____, but she couldn't tell her sister the truth — that she was going to the bowling alley to see Quentin. She had heard he was going to be there that afternoon, and she hoped to accidentally run into him. Her sister, however, continued to block the doorway.

"Get out of my way!" she demanded.

"It's my right to stand here," Kat insisted.

"Fine, but if you don't want to be a/an (3) _____ you had better forget about that right now and move!"

Again, she felt bad about being so mean to Kat. However, she couldn't explain to Kat how important it was for her to be at the bowling alley when Quentin was. She couldn't make Kat understand how cute Quentin was and how much she wanted to be his girlfriend. No, Kat had only a/an (4) _____ of knowledge about boys and wouldn't understand.

Quentin wasn't just *any* boy, anyway. He was the teenage (5) _____ of Brad Pitt and Antonio Banderas, except that he probably had a lot bigger ego than either of them. Bernadette had to admit that Quentin could be rather (6) _____, but she knew she probably would be the same way if she was as cool and good-looking as he was. Quentin was also (7) _____ for the way he treated girls. However, Bernadette knew that he would be different toward her when they started going out. She just *knew* they would be going out someday soon.

Finally, Bernadette got past her little sister and pedaled her bike as fast as she could to the bowling alley. She hoped that Quentin was still there. She decided to take a shortcut through a field just to get there more quickly. However, as she came out of the field onto the paved lot, her tire hit an empty bottle. She skidded sideways on her bike across the parking lot. When she finally slid to a stop, it was in a mud puddle.

She looked at her bike. The handlebars were twisted, the frame was bent in half and the seat was nowhere to be seen. The paint along one side had been (8) _____. Her shorts were torn, and she could feel the mud all over her face. Her leg had been (9) _____ by the chain, and she was bleeding.

It was right then that Quentin and all his friends swaggered out the door of the bowling alley and pointed at her.

"You know, I have an extra set of training wheels at home if you want them," Quentin laughed. "I haven't needed mine since I was five." He looked down at her and pointed to her bloody, ripped shorts. "Nice outfit," he laughed again and walked off, totally unconcerned about her injury.

Bernadette felt (10) _____. With a very red face, she got up and hobbled toward a pay phone. Suddenly, she didn't care about running into Quentin ever again — except maybe with her bike . . . riding very, very fast . . . hard . . . Before her angry thoughts got the best of her, she took a deep breath and headed home for help.

Super Challenge

Directions: Use the bonus words from the test to finish the story above.

More AbraVocabra • © 2001 Cottonwood Press, Inc. • www.cottonwoodpress.com • 800-864-4297 • Fort Collins, Colorado

Vocabulary List #18

inoculate: to inject a serum or vaccine to create immunity

- When a dog bit Jerry and the dog couldn't be found, his family had no choice but to **inoculate** him with a rabies vaccine.

- When Tonya was **inoculated** against the flu, she was surprised the needle didn't hurt that much.

sabotage: to destroy or damage a cause on purpose

- The strikers decided to **sabotage** production by removing a few nuts and bolts from the high-speed cutting machine.

- Kayla **sabotaged** the parade by letting her collection of pet rats loose right in front of the Glacier Valley Horse Club riders.

exclusive: excluding all but a chosen few; admitting only certain people to membership

- The Iguana Group was so **exclusive** that it hardly had any members.

- The salesman belonged to an **exclusive** club that only admitted people who had sold more than $100,000 worth of vacuum cleaners.

pragmatic: practical; sensible

- We need a **pragmatic** solution to this difficult problem.

- Even though buying a cashmere sweater was not the most **pragmatic** thing to do with her money, Melanie couldn't resist.

evolve: to develop or change over time

- Janice hoped her friendship with Michael would **evolve** into something more.

- Lester watched with amazement as his skinny awkward daughter **evolved** into a lovely, gracious woman.

shrewd: clever or sharp; having keen insight

- Amber is a **shrewd** businesswoman who made her first million dollars by the time she was 24 years old.

- Shawn's strategy for winning the contest was so **shrewd** that no one even came close to matching his score.

bilk: to cheat or swindle

- Gerald was in jail for **bilking** several people out of their life's savings.

- Fiona finally caught on to Daisy's tricks and decided she would never let Daisy **bilk** her out of her milk money again.

alleged: declared, but not proven

- The **alleged** murderer's case finally came to trial.

- Matthew drove the getaway car, but Hal was the **alleged** mailbox bomber.

homogenous: made up of similar or identical parts; uniform

- The convention of redheaded accordionists was a lot more **homogenous** than the convention of soccer fans.

- Looking at all the black business suits in the crowd, the candidate remembered that he was addressing a **homogenous** group of New York City lawyers.

heterogeneous: mixed; made up of different parts

- There was a time when only men went to barber shops and only women went to hair salons. Today, the clients at hair salons are a much more **heterogeneous** group.

- The class was a **heterogeneous** mixture of "A" students and "F" students.

Bonus Words

★poignant: emotionally painful or moving

- The play took such a **poignant** look at cancer that Sandy cried all the way home.

- Seeing her grandparents renew their wedding vows after fifty years of marriage was very **poignant** for Kerry.

★crux: the basic or essential thing

- "I know they would make our work easier," explained the company president, "but the **crux** of the matter is that the new computers are simply too expensive."

- Jeb's dad wanted to get to the **crux** of the problem before his son wound up in jail.

Name _____

Test

Matching

Match each word in the left column to its correct definition in the right column.

_____	1.	exclusive
_____	2.	sabotage
_____	3.	inoculate
_____	4.	bilk
_____	5.	evolve
_____	6.	heterogeneous
_____	7.	homogeneous
_____	8.	shrewd
_____	9.	pragmatic
_____	10.	alleged

a. emotionally painful or moving

b. a small rodent with a nasty disposition

c. to inject a serum or vaccine to create immunity

d. to turn around in a circle

e. mixed; made up of different parts

f. made up of similar or identical parts; uniform

g. how you say the word "milk" when you have a stuffy nose

h. to cheat or swindle

i. declared, but not proven

j. the basic or essential thing

k. clever or sharp; having keen insight

l. excluding all but a chosen few; admitting only certain people to membership

m. to develop or change over time

n. practical; sensible

o. to destroy or damage a cause on purpose

p. milk flavored with blueberry juice

★Bonus words

_____	11.	crux
_____	12.	poignant

Fill-in-the-Blank

Directions: The first 10 words listed above belong in the story below. Read the story and use the clues in the text to place each word in the correct blank space provided. You may change the form of a word to fit the story, if you need to. (For example, you might need to add *ed*, *ing*, *ly* or *s*.)

Mortimer's Mistake

Mortimer was so excited about his new idea. A company called Shady Day Deals, out of Reno, Nevada, wanted him to start selling its new product, "Old-No-More." Apparently, it was an anti-aging potion guaranteed to get rid of baldness, eliminate gray hair and smooth wrinkles. The only drawback was that Old-No-More could not be taken in pill form. Though people had to be (1) _____, they wanted so badly to stay young that they didn't mind the pain of an injection.

Mortimer's sister, Mollie Mae, was much (2) _____ than Mortimer, so she could see that the whole thing was a bad idea. "How can you be sure this (3) _____ youth enhancer really works? You don't have any proof," she warned, even though she knew her brother would never listen to her.

Mortimer thought Mollie was way too suspicious for her own good. Besides, she was always trying to (4) _____ his business deals. He knew she was behind the failure of his edible cherry-flavored newspaper business. He also blamed her for his other business failures, though it was true she had warned him not to open the "Build Your Own Burrito" restaurant across the street from Taco Bell. It was also true that she had pointed out that anyone allergic to dogs and cats should probably not open a bed and breakfast for pets. Mollie tended to be way too (5) _____ about things, in Mortimer's opinion.

Mortimer quickly read over the contract. "Mortimer Meese," it read, "is one of a/an (6) _____ group of businesses allowed to sell 'Old-No-More' in the New England States." He was thrilled. Immediately, he rented an office, advertised in the largest cities' newspapers (unfortunately neither edible nor cherry-flavored) and waited for the calls to flood in.

And sure enough, after just one week, the phone was ringing off the hook, and people were lined up outside his office. The customers were a very (7) _____ group. Some were as young as 25; others were in their 60s and up. However, all of them were there for one thing – the "fountain of youth" that Mortimer had promised in his ads.

Mortimer did a booming business for two weeks as he added up his huge profits. Mollie couldn't say another word about his failures.

Then a strange thing happened. After a few weeks, people who had received the first shots began trickling into the office with complaints. Soon the waiting room and then the hallway were full of people wanting a word or two with Mortimer. The odd thing was that this time the people made up a/an (8) _____ group. All the people who had used 'Old-No-More' had (9) _____ into plump people with flaming red hair.

"The last thing I wanted to was gain 50 pounds and have my hair turn red!" shouted one red-headed man.

"I want my money back, you fraud!" shouted another redhead.

"You (10) _____ me out of my hard-earned money, and you're going to hear from my lawyer," warned another.

Mortimer immediately got on the phone with Shady Day Deals. "Well," drawled the smooth-talking salesman on the other end, all we claimed was no wrinkles, no balding and no gray hair. Are any of them wrinkled, bald or gray-haired?"

"No," whined Mortimer, "but they are all . . ."

Click. The salesman hung up.

Mortimer stared at the angry mob in his waiting room and swallowed hard.

Super Challenge

Directions: Use the bonus words from the test to finish the story above.

Vocabulary List #19

peruse: to read or examine with great care

- "Since I am looking for a job, I always **peruse** the want-ads before I read the comics," said Jay.

- Polly **perused** her notes every night for a week before the big English test.

admonish: to caution, warn or scold mildly

- The teacher was always having to **admonish** three-year-old Katie for dumping sand on the other kids.

- Mr. Wentz **admonished** Jacob for shouting out the answer, but secretly he was pleased Jacob knew it.

loquacious: very talkative

- Renee was a good student, but her teachers always complained to her parents about how **loquacious** she was.

- Lindsay is **loquacious**, but her brother Quincy is very quiet.

vile: disgusting; repulsive

- Herbie was proud of his ability to belch the entire alphabet, but his sister thought his behavior was **vile**.

- The **vile** lyrics on the CD shocked Caleb's parents.

conjecture: a guess based on incomplete or inconclusive evidence

- The detective made a **conjecture** that the butler had done it, and it just so happened he was right.

- "I didn't do it!" cried Gretchen. "Your accusation is just a **conjecture**."

vendetta: an urge for revenge against a person or a group of people

- For the rest of his life, the former prisoner had a **vendetta** against the man whose testimony had wrongly convicted him.

- The Harrison family had a **vendetta** against the Triblehorn family that had lasted for generations.

extricate: to release or disentangle

- It took Sam 20 minutes to **extricate** his skateboard from the barbed wire fence he crashed into.

- "And how do you plan on **extricating** yourself from this mess?" Mary's dad asked sternly, after she told him she had accidentally ordered 1000 golf balls online.

passé: out-of-date; old-fashioned

- "What kind of teacher uses a word like 'swell'?" the eighth grader groaned. "It is so **passé**."

- The fashion world moves quickly. One month hip huggers are all the rage, and the next month they are **passé**.

incessant: non-stop; seemingly endless

- The noise from the jackhammer outside was **incessant**. So was Gwyneth's headache.

- The students' **incessant** whining and complaining was driving Ms. Jones crazy.

conventional: customary or traditional; conforming to accepted rules and standards

- Sierra found it hard to believe that her **conventional** parents were former hippies.

- You could scale the side of the building with suction cups strapped to your hands, but the more **conventional** way to get to the top floor would be to take the elevator.

Bonus Words

★prima donna: a conceited and temperamental person

- When Emily became head cheerleader, she became such a **prima donna** that no one could stand her.

- The actor was known as such a **prima donna** that many producers were reluctant to cast her in their movies.

★nonpartisan: not limited to any one political party

- Both Democrats and Republicans voted for the bill, making it clear that the issue was a **nonpartisan** one.

- The president wanted a **nonpartisan** investigation of the issue, so she appointed 10 Republicans and 10 Democrats to the committee.

Name _____

Test

Matching

Match each word in the left column to its correct definition in the right column.

_____ 1. conventional

_____ 2. vendetta

_____ 3. incessant

_____ 4. vile

_____ 5. extricate

_____ 6. peruse

_____ 7. admonish

_____ 8. conjecture

_____ 9. passé

_____ 10. loquacious

★Bonus words

_____ 11. nonpartisan

_____ 12. prima donna

a. very talkative

b. disgusting; repulsive

c. not limited to any one political party

d. to read or examine with great care

e. an urge for revenge against a person or a group of people

f. lovely

g. a conceited and tempermental person

h. an ignorant person who is hard to get along with

i. to caution, warn or scold mildly

j. a guess based on incomplete or inconclusive evidence

k. resembling a kangaroo

l. to release or disentangle

m. non-stop; seemingly endless

n. out of date; old-fashioned

o. customary or traditional; conforming to accepted rules and standards

p. a kind of patio

Fill-in-the-Blank

Directions: The first 10 words listed above belong in the story below. Read the story and use the clues in the text to place each word in the correct blank space provided. You may change the form of a word to fit the story, if you need to. (For example, you might need to add *ed*, *ing*, *ly* or *s*.)

Escape from Detention

Mr. Grooms sat and stared at poor Donna, who was in detention again. In all his years of teaching, Mr. Grooms had never seen a student as (1) _____ as Donna Fawcett. The girl just couldn't seem to keep her mouth shut. She talked (2) _____, through the entire class period, every day of the week, every week of the school year.

He (3) _____ Donna every day to stop talking, but she just didn't seem able to. One day, when Mr. Grooms had been up late grading papers the night before and was grumpy because of it, Donna talked so much he started fantasizing about a zipper on her mouth — a zipper that he could lock when she was in his class. Then he felt guilty for even thinking of such a thing. "I must be a/an (4) _____ human being," he thought. "What kind of teacher dreams up cruel punishments?" He sighed and, of course, gave her the more (5) _____ punishment of detention.

After school, he wondered if even that had been a good idea. He had a headache, and he wanted to go home, but he had to stay to supervise Donna's detention.

"I was thinking, Mr. Grooms," said Donna, interrupting her teacher's thoughts, "that your tie is kind of (6) _____. I mean, I know you're a teacher and you don't really care about being in style, but I just thought that maybe you would like to know. If I were that out of style, I would want to know. See, I've been (7) _____ the fashion magazines lately, and it seems like every one of them says that wide ties are "out" this season. I'm not sure why this is, but if I had to make a (8) _____, I'd say it's because they're so big and clumsy looking, not like the sleek skinny ones that Mr. Dillinger wears . . ."

As Donna continued her fashion review, Mr. Grooms tried desperately to think of a way to (9) _____ himself from the conversation. Finally, before Donna had a chance to move on to color choices, he found a way out. He excused her from the rest of detention, and Donna bounced merrily out into the hall. "Since you were always giving me detention, I was beginning to think you had a/an (10) _____ against me," she called back. "Now I see that you don't after all. That's good. That's really really good. Now think about what I was telling you about the tie. If you want, I could cut out some pictures and . . ."

Mr. Grooms shut the door . . . firmly.

Super Challenge

Directions: Use the bonus words from the test to finish the story above.

Vocabulary List #20

reconcile: to settle a quarrel or dispute

- After weeks of fighting, the sisters decided to **reconcile**, and there was peace in the family once more.

- The judge looked at the couple sternly and said, "For the sake of both your children and yourselves, you need to **reconcile** your silly differences."

memento: a souvenir; anything that serves as a reminder of something

- Selena bought a mouse-ear hat as a **memento** of her trip to Disneyland.

- Marcella's grandmother had a house full of interesting **mementos** from her years in the Peace Corps.

impaired: damaged or weakened

- Dale sits in the front row of all his classes because his hearing is **impaired**.

- Natalie hated the new building because it **impaired** her view of the ocean.

exasperate: to irritate or annoy a great deal

- Her children's constant fighting and whining continued to **exasperate** Mrs. Farnham.

- Troy was **exasperated** by his problems with algebra

ambidextrous: able to use both hands well

- "It would sure be nice to be **ambidextrous**," Julie sighed. "My right hand is sore from writing so much."

- Because he was **ambidextrous**, Bart became the best employee on the assembly line. When one hand got tired, he just switched to the other.

fanatic: someone with extreme and unreasonable enthusiasm for something

- Stephanie is such a health **fanatic** that she won't eat even one bite of birthday cake, ever.

- Mr. Malone is such a **fanatic** about germs that he sprays down his desk with Lysol every morning and every afternoon.

competent: capable or skillful

- The company hired Melody because she proved how **competent** she was.

- "Mr. Lawrence may dress funny," said the principal, "but he is a **competent** teacher."

teetotaler: someone who never drinks alcohol in any form

- Willy and Diana are **teetotalers**, so, needless to say, they did not appreciate it when Frank gave them a bottle of wine for their anniversary.

- Rex had a reputation for being a **teetotaler**, so Laura was very surprised when she saw him buying a bottle of beer.

ample: large in size

- My grandmother piled **ample** portions of everything onto my plate.

- The apartment had one room that was **ample** enough to hold all of Daniel's model airplanes.

vital: necessary or essential

- Lupe was such a **vital** part of the soccer team that after she was injured, the team began losing all its games.

- A good understanding of anatomy is **vital** if you want to be a doctor.

Bonus Words

★posthumous: taking place after death

- Mary was sad that her grandfather wasn't around to appreciate the **posthumous** award he received from the governor for his work at the clinic.

- The only photo of the outlaw the historical society could find was one taken **posthumously** — in his coffin.

★gingerly: carefully; cautiously

- Dr. Zworkle walked **gingerly** past the sleeping gorilla.

- Sarah **gingerly** handled the cactus she was repotting.

Name _____

Test

Matching

Match each word in the left column to its correct definition in the right column.

_____ 1. vital

_____ 2. fanatic

_____ 3. exasperate

_____ 4. memento

_____ 5. ambidextrous

_____ 6. impaired

_____ 7. competent

_____ 8. ample

_____ 9. teetotaler

_____ 10. reconcile

★Bonus words

_____ 11. posthumous

_____ 12. gingerly

a. carefully; cautiously

b. to settle a quarrel or dispute

c. a souvenir; anything that serves as a reminder of some-thing

d. damaged or weakened

e. to irritate or annoy a great deal

f. taking place after death

g. taking place before birth

h. able to use both hands well

i. able to use both feet well

j. someone with extreme and unreasonable enthusiasm for something

k. capable or skillful

l. necessary or essential

m. someone who never drinks alcohol in any form

n. large in size

o. to breathe out heavily

p. a small, portable speaker used by musicians

Fill-in-the-Blank

Directions: The first 10 words listed above belong in the story below. Read the story and use the clues in the text to place each word in the correct blank space provided. You may change the form of a word to fit the story, if you need to. (For example, you might need to add *ed, ing, ly* or *s*.)

The Sesame Situation

When the employees of the Freshest of the Fresh Bagel Bar went on strike, the whole bagel-loving town of Puxatoogie went mad. Just one day without bagels made Puxatoogians edgy. A full week had (1) _____ their thinking. They were making all kinds of silly mistakes, and many of them had trouble remembering things.

After two full weeks without Freshest of the Fresh, the mayor stepped in, not just because she missed her morning Amazin' Raisin with strawberry cream cheese on top, but because she realized what a/an (2) _____ part of the town Freshest of the Fresh really was.

Freshest of the Fresh was the people's meeting place, their forum. The school board met there every Tuesday, and the Presbyterian Women's Auxiliary Bridge Club gathered there on Thursdays. The town's many (3) _____ loved the place because it served only lemonade, iced tea and coffee. Questions about city government were discussed over garlic cream cheese on rye bagels, and solutions always emerged. For example, it was at the Freshest of the Fresh that citizens decided that the city should put in a stoplight at the corner of Third and Colorado. The City Council had no choice but to approve the money.

The strike had begun in a disagreement over sesame seed bagels. The owners of Freshest of the Fresh required that exactly 133 sesame seeds be hand-placed on each sesame seed bagel. They were absolute (4) _____ about the requirement. They would not accept one seed more or less. However, the employees, who were very (5) _____ in every other area of their jobs, could not seem to count out exactly 133 sesame seeds for every bagel. Some bagels had 132 seeds; others had 131. Some even had 134. "We don't have time to count out all these sesame seeds," the employees complained. "That much counting would (6) _____ anybody, even the most patient person in the world. It would help if we were (7) _____, but even being able to use both hands wouldn't make it that much easier."

The mayor knew she had to do something about the sesame situation, and she had to do it quickly. She picked up the phone and called the local newspaper. The next morning the headline ran: "Sesame seed situation! Emergency town meeting tonight!"

That night every single Puxatoogian showed up at the fountain in City Park, forming quite a large crowd. Although the mayor had thought there was (8) _____ room in the square, people were packed in like sardines. They were also so mad that an angry energy filled the air.

The meeting lasted six hours. The owners repeated their demands. The employees repeated theirs. Arguing broke out among the townspeople. An agreement seemed impossible.

Finally, around midnight, the mayor offered a solution. The town could try to sell the new stoplight at Third and Colorado to pay for a super-sensitive, state-of-the-art scale that would measure out the weight of exactly 133 sesame seeds. There would be no more need for counting.

The employees were ecstatic. The owners were overjoyed. At last, after several weeks of fighting, the two sides (9) _____. The headline of the next day's issue of the Puxatoogie Gazette screamed, "Sesame situation solved!" Many people put away that newspaper headline as a/an (10) _____ of the great Puxatoogie Bagel Battle.

Super Challenge

Directions: Use the bonus words from the test to finish the story above.

	1	2	3	4	5	6	7	8
V	priority	incessant	jejune*	peruse	impaired	exclusive	ambidextrous	lacerate
O	ataractic*	haughty	pragmatic	competent	epiglottis*	conventional	homogenous	conjecture
C	vile	kudzu*	prima donna	inoculate	vital	tainted	ample	hackamore*
A	evolve	sabotage	anachronism	retort	alleged	vendetta	poignant	posthumous
B	nonpartisan	extricate	blatherskite*	exasperate	notorious	martyr	memento	loquacious
R	equivalent	fanatic	bilk	heterogeneous	gingerly	flummery*	degrading	teetotaler
A	shrewd	quiddity*	admonish	obliterate	crux	passe	reconcile	smattering

Vocabulary List #21

sauté: to fry lightly in a shallow pan

- Shanelle meant to **sauté** the onions, but she wound up burning them to a crisp.

- After Nick began to **sauté** the garlic, the entire house smelled delicious.

astounded: greatly surprised or amazed

- Mr. Lucero was **astounded** when his students handed in all their assignments early.

- Jamal didn't remember entering the sweepstakes, so he was **astounded** when he won.

inhospitable: unfriendly

- The hotel staff was extremely **inhospitable**, so the group decided to leave.

- Marjorie was the most **inhospitable** restaurant hostess anyone had ever seen.

elude: to avoid, evade or escape from

- The children always tried to **elude** their Aunt Kate's welcoming kisses.

- The cat **eluded** the puppy by racing up a tree and refusing to come down for hours.

reputable: well thought of; honorable; reliable

- The Gormans thought they were ordering from a **reputable** company and were quite surprised at the poor quality of the merchandise they received.

- Despite his name, Sly Slim Cheatums was actually a **reputable** car salesman.

irrational: unreasonable; illogical

- When it came to the subject of her boyfriend, Christina was so **irrational** that she refused to believe anything at all negative about him, despite the mounting evidence that he was a liar.

- The newspaper article made the speaker sound **irrational**, but most of the audience members thought she made some excellent points.

squabble: a quarrel over a silly or trivial matter

- Last night involved a bit of a **squabble** between my sister and brother over whose turn it was to set the table.

- Myron and Malcolm were always **squabbling** about what pictures should be taped inside their locker.

tweak: a twisting pinch

- Jacqueline received a **tweak** on the ear from her mother when her response to Aunt Sydney was a bit sarcastic.

- Sometimes if you **tweak** the handle to the right a little, it will fall into place.

deem: to think, believe or judge

- To **deem** someone as a reckless driver without ever riding with him is a bit unfair.

- Much to everyone's surprise, the committee **deemed** Eric worthy of the award, despite his many arrests.

livid: extremely angry

- Derrick's mom was usually easygoing, but when Derrick made a sexist comment about girls being no good at sports, she was **livid**.

- "I was **livid**," Gina ranted. "How could Steven stand me up like that?"

Bonus Words

★skeptic: one who always questions or doubts conclusions

- "I wanted to take Aunt Clara to the séance," said Carla, "but I decided that a **skeptic** like her would have ruined all the fun."

- Though everyone else was ready to accept the conclusions of the survey, Henry was a **skeptic** and thought the study was flawed.

★embellish: to improve or touch up by adding details, often false ones

- "I wish you wouldn't **embellish** your stories," Rosa said. "They just end up sounding ridiculous."

- David heard the rumor and then **embellished** it with even more damaging details.

Name _____

Test

Matching

Match each word in the left column to its correct definition in the right column.

_____ 1. elude

_____ 2. reputable

_____ 3. astounded

_____ 4. livid

_____ 5. sauté

_____ 6. inhospitable

_____ 7. irrational

_____ 8. tweak

_____ 9. deem

_____ 10. squabble

★Bonus words

_____ 11. skeptic

_____ 12. embellish

a. unfriendly

b. one who always questions or doubts conclusions

c. a twisting pinch

d. extremely angry

e. a large speaker

f. where you stay when you're very sick

g. to avoid, evade or escape from

h. greatly surprised or amazed

i. to think, believe or judge

j. a fight between two turkeys

k. to fry lightly in a shallow pan

l. a quarrel over a silly or trivial matter

m. to improve or touch up by adding details, often false ones

n. unreasonable; illogical

o. well thought of; honorable; reliable

p. a six-day week

Fill-in-the-Blank

Directions: The first 10 words listed above belong in the story below. Read the story and use the clues in the text to place each word in the correct blank space provided. You may change the form of a word to fit the story, if you need to. (For example, you might need to add *ed, ing, ly* or *s*.)

Food For Thought

Mr. and Mrs. Lantz were (1) _____ when they met their daughter's date, Derek. His hair was dyed bright orange in a single line from his forehead to the back of his neck. The rest of his head was purple. Immediately, they (2) _____ him unsuitable for their daughter. They reluctantly invited him in, but then they were downright (3) _____ to him. In fact, they refused to let Andrea leave with him.

Andrea was (4) _____. "You can't judge a person by his hair style!" she cried. "How could you be so (5) _____? You always tell me that looks aren't important and that it's what's inside that counts. Then you judge Derek by looking at only his hair. You don't know a thing about him!"

Mrs. Lantz tried to listen, and she realized that Andrea had a point. Her argument made a lot of sense. Mr. Lantz, however, held his ground. "He has to be an idiot!" he shouted. "Only an idiot would wear orange and purple hair."

"He's not an idiot," she said firmly.

"How do you know?" her father answered. "He can't possibly have a job, since I'm sure no one would ever hire someone who looks like him."

"You're wrong," said Andrea. "He has quite a (6) _____ job. He's a calculus tutor at the college."

"Why would the college hire a fifteen-year-old as a tutor?" Mr. Lantz asked. He wasn't buying the story.

"Because he's so smart," said Andrea. "He's also a great cook and wants to be a chef someday. How about if I bring him over and let him make dinner for us?"

"We'll be poisoned for sure," said Mr. Lantz.

"Calm down, dear," said Mrs. Lantz. "Let's let the boy cook us dinner." She was really sick of cooking.

Mr. Lantz scowled, but it was agreed that Derek would cook dinner. There was a little bit of a (7) _____ about what time to have the dinner, but finally everyone agreed to 7:00 on Thursday.

When Mr. Lantz came home on Thursday night, Derek had been (8) _____ garlic, and a wonderful aroma filled the air. Mr. Lantz relaxed just a little. The dinner *did* smell good. He (9) _____ his little beagle's ear affectionately, sat down in his recliner and tried to read the newspaper. A mosquito started buzzing around his head, though, annoying him. He tried and tried to swat the bug, but it always managed to (10) _____ him. By the time dinner was ready, he was really aggravated. He walked into the dining room, and there was Derek.

His hair was no longer purple and orange. It was emerald green and magenta. Mr. Lantz exploded.

"What is *wrong* with you?" he cried.

"Here, Dad," said Andrea, putting a spoonful of shrimp scampi to his lips.

He swallowed.

He smiled.

He sat down and looked eagerly at the pan of shrimp scampi.

"Um . . . maybe green and magenta hair isn't so bad," he mumbled. He really, really loved shrimp scampi.

Super Challenge

Directions: Use the bonus words from the test to finish the story above.

More AbraVocabra • © 2001 Cottonwood Press, Inc. • www.cottonwoodpress.com • 800-864-4297 • Fort Collins, Colorado

Vocabulary List #22

potential: possibility; ability to succeed

- When Thomas ran three miles without getting tired, the coach could see his **potential** as a long distance runner.

- A good teacher sees the **potential** in every student.

molten: melted or liquified by heat

- The islanders left their village before the **molten** lava started flowing down the volcano.

- Chef LaRuse poured the **molten** cheese over the warm croissants.

poach: to hunt illegally

- Mark was so hungry he decided to creep into the woods at night and **poach** a deer.

- The farmer was very angry about the hunters who were **poaching** on his property and endangering him and his family.

sincere: honest; straightforward and truthful

- My best friend, Hannah, is always **sincere** in her compliments to others.

- Tyrone knew the salesman wasn't **sincere** about his promises because they were just too good to be true.

revive: to bring back to consciousness

- Lana **revived** the Amazing Splashman after he made his daring cliff dive into the ocean and swallowed too much water.

- The dog appeared to be dead, but the veterinarian managed to **revive** him.

veteran: a person who has served in the armed forces

- Edward, a **veteran** of World War I, has incredible stories of his years in combat.

- My grandfather met with others **veterans** who had survived the famous battle.

rookie: a new recruit; an inexperienced person

- The **rookie** on Ted's miniature golf team made a serious mistake when he tried to putt through the giant plastic clown head.

- **Rookie** police officers often make mistakes, but they soon learn by experience what they should and shouldn't do.

competitor: a rival; a person who competes

- The school's **competitors** in football are the Brighton Bulldozers and the Fenway Falcons.

- Pete considered the guy with the 1957 Chevy to be his ultimate **competitor** when it came to the midnight drag races.

windfall: unexpected good fortune

- The inheritance was a **windfall** that helped Lavita start her own non-profit organization, People for the Fair Treatment of Mosquitos.

- Gregory is constantly blessed with **windfalls** that manage to pull him out of debt.

gorge: to eat a lot of food in a short period of time; to devour greedily

- If you **gorge** yourself on junk food, you won't be hungry for dinner.

- The giant sat in the orchard, **gorging** himself on great handfuls of plums.

Bonus Words

★assiduous: done with constant and careful attention; determined and persistent

- Max and Cassandra were **assiduous** in their search for the perfect home to buy.

- Mary is so **assiduous** about recording the weather that she can tell you the exact temperature, morning or evening, for any day in the last 25 years.

★flounder: to struggle awkwardly to move; to stumble about in a confused manner

- Everyone was surprised when Pamela fell on the ski run and began to **flounder** in the deep snow.

- Fido **floundered** in the mud as he tried to get out of the pond.

Name _____

Test

Matching

Match each word in the left column to its correct definition in the right column.

_____ 1. rookie

_____ 2. competitor

_____ 3. molten

_____ 4. gorge

_____ 5. potential

_____ 6. sincere

_____ 7. revive

_____ 8. poach

_____ 9. windfall

_____ 10. veteran

★Bonus words

_____ 11. assiduous

_____ 12. flounder

a. to hunt illegally

b. a rival; a person who competes

c. possibility; ability to succeed

d. to eat a lot of food in a short period of time; to devour greedily

e. to bake

f. a person who has served in the armed forces

g. unexpected good fortune

h. to struggle awkwardly to move; to stumble about in a confused manner

i. a doctor who treats sick and injured animals

j. a new recruit; an inexperienced person

k. melted or liquified by heat

l. to bring back to consciousness

m. done with constant and careful attention; determined and persistent

n. something destroyed in a storm

o. honest; straightforward and truthful

Fill-in-the-Blank

Directions: The first 10 words listed above belong in the story below. Read the story and use the clues in the text to place each word in the correct blank space provided. You may change the form of a word to fit the story, if you need to. (For example, you might need to add *ed, ing, ly* or *s*.)

The Secret Ingredient

Willard, a Vietnam War (1) _____, became a game warden after he got out of the army, and he stayed in the position for many years. He enjoyed his work. He liked catching people who illegally (2) _____ on public land, and he always tried to make sure they received appropriate punishment. Sometimes he was able to help injured animals. Once, for example, he helped (3) _____ a moose that had stumbled and knocked itself out.

Willard's real passion, however, was cooking chili. He loved chili, and he loved cooking it. Every year he competed in the county Crackpot Chili Cook-Off, and he had won first place for fifteen years in a row. Then, last year, a/an (4) _____ moved in and edged him out of first place. Willard was crushed. He moped around for days. Then, suddenly, his grandfather died, and Willard inherited a lot of money. Because of the (5) _____, he decided to quit his job as game warden and work on his chili, full time.

Soon, Willard had come up with a secret ingredient. He knew that no one would be able to beat him out of the first place prize, which was a lifetime supply of cornbread.

On the day of the Cook-Off, Willard walked through the aisles, smelling the wonderfully spicy scents and watching people sample various kinds of chili. His booth was already set up and he was just taking a stroll while his chili simmered. People all over were buzzing with excitement. They couldn't wait to start (6) _____ themselves on delicious bowls of chili.

When he returned to his booth, Willard noticed that a new competitor had set up a booth right next to him and was attracting a lot of attention. People were lining up to get his chili. Willard squeezed in between a few people to see what all the fuss was about and then he saw it. This guy was no (7) _____; he knew exactly what he was doing. Willard watched as people sprinkled handfuls of cheese on the tops of their heaping bowls of chili and his mouth drooled as he looked at the (8) _____ cheddar. The smell was incredible. People were saying that this chili had definite (9) _____ and might even be a winner. Of course, the judges would never allow the sprinkling of cheese during the official tasting, but it was a good strategy to attract attention to his booth and get people talking. The judges would be sure to hear about the chili's popularity. It might even affect their judgment. Though his competitor was making him very nervous, Willard still walked over, shook his hand, and congratulated him on his strategy. He was (10) _____ in his praise. After all, it *was* a good idea.

It wouldn't be good enough, though. He went to his own stove and added more of his secret ingredient — 12 cups more. After all, he thought, "You can't have too much of a good thing!"

Unfortunately, he was wrong. As the judges gobbled antacid tablets and gave Willard dirty looks, he knew how wrong he had been.

Super Challenge

Directions: Use the bonus words from the test to finish the story above.

Vocabulary List #23

cringe: to draw back in fear or pain

- Needles make George **cringe**.
- Lisa had to **cringe** when she watched the skier tumble down the snowy cliff.

nurture: to raise; to nourish, educate or train

- Pedro decided to **nurture** the kitten his daughter found in the alley.
- Alexandra **nurtured** her sister's five children after she and her husband died in a car accident.

brawl: a noisy fight

- The old western included a saloon **brawl** between the guys in white hats and the guys in black hats.
- A **brawl** started in the stadium when the home football team lost the game.

jaunt: a short trip for pleasure

- The friends took a **jaunt** out to the lake so they could paddle around in their canoe.
- Mr. Haratun was tired of chopping wood, so he took a little **jaunt** into town to see a movie.

bland: dull and tasteless

- Marta complained that the salad was **bland** without peppers.
- Leroy's grandfather will eat only **bland** foods because he has trouble with his digestion.

envious: jealous over someone else's good fortune

- Whenever Dora looked at her neighbor's beautiful rose garden, she couldn't help comparing it to her own sickly-looking plants and feeling a little **envious**.
- James was so **envious** of his brother that he couldn't bear to congratulate him on his national win.

celebrity: a famous person

- Cameras clicked and flashed as the **celebrity** made her entrance.
- Ling wanted to star on a soap opera and become a television **celebrity**.

aromatic: sweet smelling; fragrant

- Cecilia always wore an **aromatic** perfume that reminded her husband of the ocean.
- The **aromatic** bread baking in the oven made the house seem safe and cozy.

lurk: to sneak around or hide in order to attack

- Colin was always on the alert because his sister liked to **lurk** behind the sofa, jumping out and scaring him when he stumbled to breakfast half asleep.
- The tiger sensed the hunters **lurking** in the bushes.

edible: fit to be eaten

- Octopus may not look **edible**, but many people find it delicious.
- Susan refuses to believe that snails are **edible**.

Bonus Words

★secular: having to do with the ordinary, rather than the religious or spiritual

- There are many examples of beautiful music, both sacred and **secular**.
- In order to nurture one's spirit, it is sometimes necessary to retreat from the **secular** world.

★quirky: eccentric; peculiar; odd or unusual

- Simon had a few **quirky** personality traits, but they didn't bother Anne-Marie a bit.
- Savannah had a **quirky** way of dressing that attracted attention wherever she went.

Name _____

Test

Matching

Match each word in the left column to its correct definition in the right column.

_____ 1. jaunt

_____ 2. envious

_____ 3. lurk

_____ 4. edible

_____ 5. aromatic

_____ 6. celebrity

_____ 7. cringe

_____ 8. bland

_____ 9. nurture

_____ 10. brawl

a. to draw back in fear or pain

b. fit to be eaten

c. to sneak around or hide in order to attack

d. a noisy fight

e. a vine-like plant that often grows on buildings

f. eccentric; peculiar; odd or unusual

g. a metal piece that holds a door on a frame

h. a short trip for pleasure

i. to raise; to nourish, educate or train

j. not having to do with religion

k. dull and tasteless

l. easily fooled

m. sweet smelling; fragrant

n. jealous over someone else's good fortune

o. a famous person

p. inspired with love

q. hungry

★Bonus words

_____ 11. secular

_____ 12. quirky

Fill-in-the-Blank

Directions: The first 10 words listed above belong in the story below. Read the story and use the clues in the text to place each word in the correct blank space provided. You may change the form of a word to fit the story, if you need to. (For example, you might need to add *ed*, *ing*, *ly* or *s*.)

The Chef Pepe Incident

Pepe the chef was quite the (1) _____ in the little town of Moose Crossing. He had come to the Gourmet Club restaurant from Washington, D.C., where he had once worked in the White House. His dishes were more than just (2) _____. They were the best for miles around, and his restaurant was the most popular. It even had a bakery, which was so (3) _____ that passersby quickly developed an appetite and had to come in for a creme puff or a slice of cake or pie.

The problem was that Pepe would not share his recipes with anyone. No matter how much people begged, or how much they offered to pay him, he wouldn't share his secrets.

A man named Erasmus Heatherington just wouldn't give up trying to figure out Chef Pepe's recipes. He ate at the Gourmet Club every single breakfast, lunch and dinner for two months, tasting everything carefully and taking notes. Then he would go home and try to make the same dishes. Instead of being delicious like Chef Pepe's, however, they always tasted (4) _____. Erasmus was so (5) _____ he just couldn't stand it. Why why, why couldn't he cook like Chef Pepe?

He began (6) _____ around the restaurant after it closed, peeking in windows and trying to discover what made Chef Pepe's dishes so different from his own. Once he cut his foot on some broken glass and (7) _____ when he saw the blood. He hated blood.

Chef Pepe saw the blood in the alley the next morning. "Hmmmm . . ." he thought. "It looks like those creeps at the bar next door got into a/an (8) _____ again." He sighed and went back to work, thinking that it might be a good idea to move the location of his restaurant. Strange things had been happening lately. He sometimes felt like he was being watched, and he certainly didn't like the idea of having violent people around.

To cheer himself up, he took a little (9) _____ to the country, to his onion farm. There he grew the secret ingredient that made all his food so delicious. It was a special kind of onion he had imported from an island in the South Pacific. It made spicy dishes taste spicier and sweet dishes taste sweeter. It was magic. It took a lot of time and energy to (10) _____ the onions, but all the trouble was worth it. One tablespoon of them could make any ordinary recipe in the world taste perfect, absolutely perfect.

Chef Pepe smiled. Erasmus Heatherington was never going to figure it out.

Super Challenge

Directions: Use the bonus words from the test to finish the story, above.

Vocabulary List #24

distinguished: worthy of special recognition or honor; prominent

- The president announced, "We are proud to have such a **distinguished** panel here with us today."

- Professor Georgina Dunlap was a **distinguished** scientist known for her research on the behavior of the marmoset.

immigrant: a person who comes to a new country and settles there

- The Irish **immigrants** brought many old Irish traditions to the neighborhood where Erin grew up.

- The Leszynskis are **immigrants** who wasted no time founding the Polish Accordion Club in their new neighborhood.

legible: capable of being read

- Principal Potter had to redo all the diplomas for the 6th grade class because the student's names were not **legible**.

- The pharmacist always liked receiving prescriptions from Dr. Madsen because his signature was the only one he ever saw that was **legible**.

heritage: traditions, customs and/or beliefs passed down from ancestors

- Frederick wanted to learn more about his Russian **heritage**, so he paid close attention to his grandfather's stories.

- "I am proud of my Mexican **heritage**," smiled Rosa as she addressed the children at the fiesta.

partial: incomplete; not total

- Since Jeremy hadn't read the chapter, he was lucky that he could give even a **partial** answer to the question on the test.

- Roxanne made a **partial** payment, hoping that would satisfy the credit card company until her tax refund came in.

slogan: a catchy phrase used to advertise a product

- "Pamper your puppy at Perky's" was the **slogan** for Perky's Puppy Place.

- Samantha stood in the doorway listening to her parents and their friends remembering **slogans** from their childhood for products that she had never heard of.

underdog: the one expected to lose a contest

- Jessica always cheers for the **underdog** when she watches sports.

- Although Jeff's football team was considered the **underdog**, it came from behind to win.

staff: the people who work for a business

- Since Valentine's Day was coming, the **staff** at Fufu's Flowers and Candygrams had to work overtime.

- "The **staff** at Finest Friendly Folks truly is the finest," declared Merlin.

feeble: weak; not forceful; ineffective

- The dog fell into the creek after making a **feeble** attempt to jump across it.

- He made such a **feeble** effort to win the race that no one believed he cared about winning.

snide: sarcastic; mean; intended as a put-down

- The saleswoman at the elite dress shop made a **snide** remark as she looked at the customer's shabby dress.

- The chairman's **snide** comments were making him quite unpopular with the other members.

Bonus Words

★pithy: short but full of meaning

- After the long-winded speech by the principal, the audience was grateful for the guest speaker's **pithy** remarks.

- Mike never said much during a game, but he always had a **pithy** comment at the end.

★brazen: bold; shameless

- Jeffrey's **brazen** remarks about the superintendent shocked everyone at the meeting.

- The group made a **brazen** attempt to steal one of the paintings as the television crew filmed the opening of the exhibition.

Name _____

Test

Matching

Match each word in the left column to its correct definition in the right column.

_____ 1. underdog

_____ 2. staff

_____ 3. legible

_____ 4. feeble

_____ 5. immigrant

_____ 6. partial

_____ 7. slogan

_____ 8. heritage

_____ 9. distinguished

_____ 10. snide

★Bonus words

_____ 11. brazen

_____ 12. pithy

a. wobbly

b. the hard seed found in the center of some fruits

c. a person who comes to a new country and settles there

d. capable of being read

e. the people who work for a business

f. worthy of special recognition or honor; prominent

g. short but full of meaning

h. weak; not forceful; ineffective

i. bold; shameless

j. sarcastic; mean; intended as a put-down

k. the one expected to lose a contest

l. traditions, customs and/or beliefs passed down from ancestors

m. incomplete; not total

n. seared to seal in the flavor

o. a catchy phrase used to advertise a product

p. goggles

Fill-in-the-Blank

Directions: The first 10 words listed above belong in the story below. Read the story and use the clues in the text to place each word in the correct blank space provided. You may change the form of a word to fit the story, if you need to. (For example, you might need to add *ed, ing, ly* or *s*.)

Bip's Bellows

The sun was shining when Bip Pemberton, a/an (1) _____ from Shepplemania, arrived in the town of Blokesville, a quiet little village on the sea. The people in the town had never seen someone from Shepplemania and didn't know what to expect. They were willing to give Bip Pemberton a chance, however, because they had always respected a person's (2) _____. "Our roots are important!" they always said.

Bip decided to open a music store, specializing in the accordion. (He had been known as a/an (3) _____ accordion player in Shepplemania, but he knew that in his new town he would have to earn that respect all over again.) He found a store to lease, and the landlord allowed him to make a/an (4) _____ payment in order to hold the place until he could get the rest from his bank in Shepplemania. Then he hired a sign painter. He would have painted the sign himself, but he knew it wouldn't be (5) _____ if he painted it. He had terrible handwriting. As soon as he picked up the finished sign, he hung it above the store and smiled. "Bip's Bellows," he read proudly.

Bip quickly hired a small (6) _____ of four people and opened the store. He was very proud of his new business. He often repeated his (7) _____, which was, "If you haven't heard an accordion, you haven't lived." On weekends, while the staff covered the store, he would take his accordion to the beach and play songs for the volleyball players and the sand castle builders. At first, some people made (8) _____ remarks about "the squeezebox" and insulted Bip in their (9) _____ attempts to be funny. Then Bip entered the county talent contest.

Every year for 10 years, Ella Crungley had won the contest with a number that involved baton twirling and her seven tap dancing poodles. She was a very popular performer, so Bip knew he was a/an (10) _____. He decided to enter anyway. He wrote a song especially for the contest. The song was called "Super-Duper Blokesville."

As he played the song at the talent show, he crowd went wild. He won. Soon teenagers all over Blokesville were putting aside their drums and guitars and begging their parents for accordions.

Bip was very, very happy.

Super Challenge

Directions: Use the bonus words from the test to finish the story above.

	1	2	3	4	5	6	7	8
V	quirky	elude	deem	firkin*	jaunt	molten	underdog	edible
O	irrational	competitor	sauté	aromatic	wombat*	heritage	lurk	astounded
C	legible	panegyric*	potential	secular	veteran	normoblast*	distinguished	embellish
A	skeptic	feeble	bland	tweak	staff	brawl	slogan	nurture
B	brazen	assiduous	rallentando*	immigrant	windfall	inhospitable	revive	partial
R	parbuckle*	reputable	celebrity	poach	pithy	cringe	envious	rookie
A	sincere	livid	gorge	flounder	tektite*	snide	squabble	shalloon*

Appendix

Alphabetical List of All Words in More AbraVocabra

Regular Words

accumulate	colossal	essential	inadequate
adjacent	commend	euphemism	incessant
admonish	competent	evolve	indelible
affable	competitor	exasperate	indigent
alleged	compulsory	exclusive	inept
alternative	condescending	exempt	inevitable
ambidextrous	conjecture	expletive	inhabited
ambitious	contemplate	exposé	inhospitable
ample	conventional	extravagant	inoculate
animosity	credentials	extricate	insinuate
anonymous	cringe	fanatic	instinct
apathetic	decisive	feeble	irrational
apprehensive	deem	fluctuate	irreverent
aromatic	defer	frail	jaunt
ashen	defiant	fraud	jeopardy
astounded	degrading	frugal	juvenile
authoritarian	deluge	fundamental	lacerate
barter	demented	gala	lavish
bedraggled	demure	gaudy	legendary
begrudge	deteriorate	gorge	legible
biased	deterrent	guru	lenient
bigot	devastate	haggard	literally
bilk	disclose	haggle	livid
bland	disdain	haughty	loquacious
brawl	distinguished	heathen	lurk
buffoon	dormant	heritage	manipulate
bungle	drone	heterogeneous	martyr
bustling	edible	homogenous	meander
capacity	eloquent	humdrum	memento
caricature	elude	immense	menacing
celebrity	enchanted	immigrant	modest
chic	enhance	imminent	molten
clad	enlighten	immune	morose
clamor	envious	impaired	nausea
collate	envious	imply	nestle
colleague	equivalent	improbable	nimble

nomad

notorious

nuptial

nurture

obliterate

omniscient

ostracize

pacifist

painstaking

parched

partial

passé

permeate

persistent

peruse

pervasive

petty

pilfer

pious

poach

pompous

potential

pragmatic

precarious

preliminary

priority

psychosomatic

puny

radical

reconcile

reiterate

repertoire

reprehensible

reputable

retort

reverberate

revive

revoke

rookie

rural

sabotage

sauté

scapegoat

scrutinize

shrewd

sieve

sincere

slogan

smattering

smoke screen

smolder

snide

solemn

spar

sparse

spontaneous

sporadic

sprawl

squabble

staff

stagnant

status quo

stodgy

subsequent

subtle

suffrage

superfluous

supplement

surpass

surrogate

synonymous

teetotaler

temperamental

transformation

trivial

turf

tweak

underdog

unintelligible

urban

utopia

vague

vendetta

veteran

vile

vindicate

vintage

vital

voracious

wager

whim

whimsical

windfall

wither

zany

zest

Bonus Words

adroitly

anachronism

assiduous

atrophy

behemoth

bona fide

brazen

cache

callous

chagrin

complacent

comprehensive

context

crux

debonair

embellish

fabricate

faux pas

flamboyant

flounder

formidable

gall

gingerly

hierarchy

incognito

indigo

mayhem

nebulous

nonchalant

nonpartisan

ostentatious

parody

pithy

plethora

poignant

posthumous

prima donna

quash

quirky

rendezvous

repugnant

scenario

secular

semblance

skeptic

tainted

vaudeville

vibrant

Word Lists at a Glance

Word List #1
alternative
utopia
ashen
affable
barter
exposé
irreverent
gala
ostracize
scapegoat

Bonus Words
parody
behemoth

Word List #2
whimsical
inadequate
contemplate
humdrum
vindicate
euphemism
inhabited
turf
colleague
stagnant

Bonus Words
scenario
nonchalant

Word List #3
devastate
instinct
vintage
haggard
pervasive
suffrage
condescending
status quo
reverberate
drone

Bonus Words
flamboyant
context

Word List #4
eloquent
inevitable
guru
demure
smolder
stodgy
indelible
deterrent
imply
apprehensive

Bonus Words
rendezvous
plethora

Word List #5
spar
insinuate
modest
precarious
disclose
extravagant
bustling
smoke screen
enlighten
transformation

Bonus Words
fabricate
debonair

Word List #6
compulsory
biased
radical
persistent
inept
surrogate
credentials
disdain
deluge
immune

Bonus Words
ostentatious
faux pas

Word List #7
decisive
apathetic
manipulate
exempt
revoke
defer
literally
capacity
fundamental
psychosomatic

Bonus Words
semblance
hierarchy

Word List #8
legendary
scrutinize
nomad
caricature
parched
defiant
clad
subtle
spontaneous
improbable

Bonus Words
quash
atrophy

Word List #9
supplement
collate
nestle
unintelligible
imminent
painstaking
reprehensible
gaudy
sporadic
surpass

Bonus Words
complacent
bona fide

Word List #10
deteriorate
immense
solemn
urban
vague
rural
frail
juvenile
trivial
wither

Bonus Words
indigo
vibrant

Word List #11
meander
lavish
nausea
fraud
petty
accumulate
buffoon
zany
puny
colossal

Bonus Words
vaudeville
mayhem

Word List #12
voracious
reiterate
begrudge
pacifist
omniscient
superfluous
morose
permeate
repertoire
animosity

Bonus Words
incognito
chagrin

Word List #13

subsequent
ambitious
bigot
enchanted
essential
sparse
wager
frugal
haggle
demented

Bonus Words

gall
callous

Word List #14

heathen
enhance
bungle
lenient
anonymous
zest
sprawl
sieve
envious
nimble

Bonus Words

cache
repugnant

Word List #15

dormant
nuptial
fluctuate
expletive
pompous
pilfer
indigent
commend
chic
authoritarian

Bonus Words

comprehensive
adroitly

Word List #16

preliminary
temperamental
pious
menacing
bedraggled
clamor
jeopardy
whim
adjacent
synonymous

Bonus Words

formidable
nebulous

Word List #17

smattering
priority
obliterate
haughty
degrading
retort
martyr
notorious
equivalent
lacerate

Bonus Words

tainted
anachronism

Word List #18

inoculate
sabotage
exclusive
pragmatic
evolve
shrewd
bilk
alleged
homogenous
heterogeneous

Bonus Words

poignant
crux

Word List #19

peruse
admonish
loquacious
vile
conjecture
vendetta
extricate
passé
incessant
conventional

Bonus Words

prima donna
nonpartisan

Word List #20

reconcile
memento
impaired
exasperate
ambidextrous
fanatic
competent
teetotaler
ample
vital

Bonus Words

posthumous
gingerly

Word List #21

sauté
astounded
inhospitable
elude
reputable
irrational
squabble
tweak
deem
livid

Bonus Words

skeptic
embellish

Word List #22

potential
molten
poach
sincere
revive
veteran
rookie
competitor
windfall
gorge

Bonus Words

assiduous
flounder

Word List #23

cringe
nurture
brawl
jaunt
bland
envious
celebrity
aromatic
lurk
edible

Bonus Words

secular
quirky

Word List #24

distinguished
immigrant
legible
heritage
partial
slogan
underdog
staff
feeble
snide

Bonus Words

pithy
brazen

Pieces for Vocabra Game

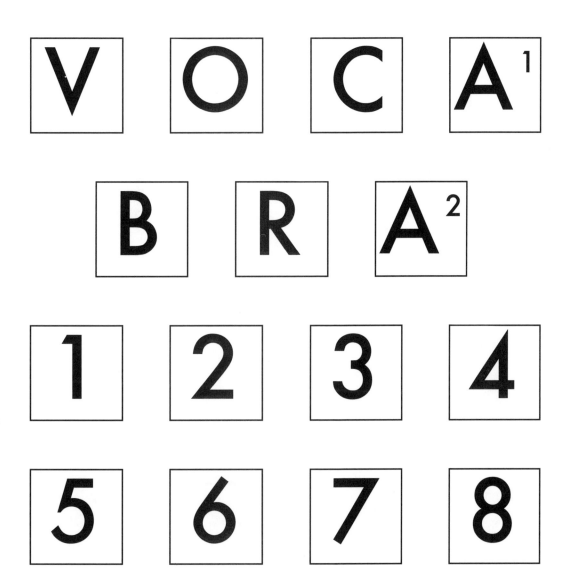

Definitions of Weird Words

Vocabra Game, Lists 1-4

ocellus: a small, simple eye common to invertebrates; an eyelike colored spot on an animal or on a leaf of a plant

quotidian: occurring every day; commonplace, ordinary

rodomontade: pretentious boasting or bragging; bluster

flummox: to confuse; perplex

punctilious: attentive to the finer points of etiquette and formal conduct

flapdoodle: foolish talk; nonsense

lollygag: to fool around; to spend time aimlessly; to dawdle or dally

oyez: used three times in succession to introduce the opening of a court of law; a call to attention

Vocabra Game, Lists 5-8

malapropism: the usually unintentionally humorous misuse or distortion of a word or phrase; especially: the use of a word sounding somewhat like the one intended but ludicrously wrong in the context

quidnunc: a nosy person; a busybody

malarkey: exaggerated or meaningless talk; nonsense

palaver: idle chatter

paronomasia: word play; especially a pun

clerihew: a humorous poem about a person who is generally named in the first line

scombroid: of or belonging to the suborder Scombroidei, which includes marine fishes such as the mackerel

punka: a fan used especially in India, made of a palm frond or strip of cloth hung from the ceiling and moved by a servant

Vocabra Game, Lists 9-12

oology: the study of birds' eggs

salmagundi: any mixture or assortment; a potpourri

quixotic: caught up in the romance of noble deeds or unreachable ideals; romantic without regard to practicality

albedo: the white, spongy inner lining of a citrus fruit rind

manticore: a fabulous monster having the head of a man, body of a lion, and the tail of a dragon or scorpion

palooka: an incompetent or easily defeated player, especially a prize fighter

thrasonical: boastful

hallux: the inner or first digit on the hind foot of a mammal; in man, the big toe

Vocabra Game, Lists 13-16

burgomaster: in the Netherlands, Flanders, Austria, and Germany, the principal magistrate of a city or town, comparable to a mayor

incunabulum: a book printed from movable type before 1501; an artifact of an early period

flabbergast: to make speechless with amazement; astonish

mondegreen: creative mishearing of song lyrics

grommet: an eyelet, as of metal or plastic, protecting an opening in cloth, leather, etc.

maelstrom: a powerful, often violent whirlpool sucking in objects within a given radius; a situation that resembles such a whirlpool in violence, turbulence, or power to engulf katzenjammer: a loud discordant noise; a state of depression or bewilderment

palimpsest: a written document, typically on parchment, that has been written upon several times, often with remnants of earlier, imperfectly erased writing still visible

Vocabra Game, Lists 17-20

quiddity: the real nature of a thing; essence

ataractic: pertaining to or conducive of calmness or peace of mind

epiglottis: an elastic cartilage located at the root of the tongue that folds over the glottis to prevent food from entering the windpipe during the act of swallowing

flummery: any of several soft, light, bland foods, such as custard or jelly.

jejune: not nourishing; insubstantial

blatherskite: a babbling, foolish person; absurd and foolish talk

kudzu: a vine, native to Japan, having compound leaves and clusters of reddish-purple flowers and grown for fodder and forage

hackamore: a rope or rawhide halter with a wide band that can be lowered over a horse's eyes, used in breaking horses to a bridle

Vocabra Game, Lists 21-24

normoblast: an immature red blood cell, characterized by abundant hemoglobin and a small nucleus

tektite: any of numerous dark brown to green glass objects, generally small and rounded, theorized to be of extraterrestrial origin, found chiefly in Czechoslovakia, Australia, Indonesia, the Philippines, Texas and Georgia, and having a largely silica composition with various oxides

wombat: either of two Australian marsupials, somewhat resembling small bears

panegyric: a formal speech or piece of writing praising a person or event

shalloon: a lightweight wool or worsted twill fabric, used chiefly for coat linings

parbuckle: a rope sling for rolling cylindrical objects up and down an inclined plane

rallentando: a musical term meaning a gradual slackening in tempo

firkin: a small wooden barrel or keg, used especially for storing butter, cheese, or lard

Test Answer Keys

List #1, Answer Key

Matching
1. h
2. i
3. b
4. c
5. j
6. g
7. o
8. f
9. n
10. a

Bonus Words
11. l
12. d

Fill-in-the-blank
1. utopia
2. affable
3. irreverent
4. gala
5. barter
6. exposé
7. ashen
8. scapegoat
9. alternative
10. ostracized

Super Challenge
Answers will vary.

List #2, Answer Key

Matching
1. m
2. i
3. a
4. l
5. o
6. k
7. b
8. d
9. e
10. h

Bonus Words
11. f
12. n

Fill-in-the-blank
1. humdrum
2. colleagues
3. inhabited
4. contemplating
5. whimsical
6. vindicate
7. euphemism
8. turf
9. stagnant
10. inadequate

Super Challenge
Answers will vary.

List #3, Answer Key

Matching
1. j
2. a
3. n
4. b
5. i
6. h
7. o
8. e
9. m
10. g

Bonus Words
11. k
12. d

Fill-in-the-blank
1. vintage
2. suffrage
3. reverberated
4. drone
5. pervasive
6. haggard
7. condescending
8. devastate
9. status quo
10. instinct

Super Challenge
Answers will vary.

List #4, Answer Key

Matching
1. h
2. e
3. d
4. m
5. k
6. j
7. o
8. c
9. f
10. b

Bonus Words
11. n
12. a

Fill-in-the-blank
1. demure
2. gurus
3. stodgy
4. eloquent
5. apprehensive
6. smoldering
7. implying
8. inevitable
9. deterrent
10. indelible

Super Challenge
Answers will vary.

List #5, Answer Key

Matching	Fill-in-the-blank
1. j	1. bustling
2. l	2. precariously
3. b	3. insinuating
4. m	4. smoke screen
5. n	5. sparring
6. i	6. extravagant
7. o	7. enlighten
8. a	8. disclose
9. c	9. transformation
10. k	10. modest
Bonus Words	
11. f	
12. g	

Super Challenge
Answers will vary.

List #6, Answer Key

Matching	Fill-in-the-blank
1. j	1. radical
2. k	2. deluge
3. h	3. immune
4. e	4. persistent
5. g	5. credentials
6. n	6. inept
7. d	7. surrogate
8. o	8. disdain
9. i	9. biased
10. c	10. compulsory
Bonus Words	
11. m	
12. a	

Super Challenge
Answers will vary.

List #7, Answer Key

Matching

1. g
2. n
3. f
4. k
5. a
6. d
7. m
8. h
9. l
10. c

Bonus Words

11. e
12. o

Fill-in-the-blank

1. exempt
2. defer
3. decisive
4. revoke
5. fundamental
6. apathetic
7. psychosomatic
8. literally
9. capacity
10. manipulated

Super Challenge

Answers will vary.

List #8, Answer Key

Matching

1. n
2. e
3. l
4. i
5. g
6. c
7. m
8. b
9. o
10. h

Bonus Words

11. a
12. d

Fill-in-the-blank

1. legendary
2. nomads
3. clad
4. parched
5. spontaneously
6. subtle
7. improbable
8. scrutinized
9. defiantly
10. caricature

Super Challenge

Answers will vary.

List #9, Answer Key

Matching
1. o
2. l
3. k
4. e
5. f
6. n
7. d
8. b
9. a
10. h

Bonus Words
11. i
12. c

Fill-in-the-blank
1. nestled
2. sporadically
3. reprehensible
4. collated
5. painstaking
6. gaudy
7. surpassed
8. supplement
9. unintelligible
10. imminent

Super Challenge
Answers will vary.

List #10, Answer Key

Matching
1. b
2. n
3. d
4. h
5. k
6. m
7. j
8. f
9. a
10. o

Bonus Words
11. l
12. e

Fill-in-the-blank
1. withered
2. frail
3. rural
4. urban
5. vague
6. deteriorated
7. trivial
8. immense
9. solemn
10. juvenile

Super Challenge
Answers will vary.

List #11, Answer Key

Matching
1. i
2. j
3. h
4. c
5. n
6. f
7. b
8. k
9. g
10. a

Bonus Words
11. o
12. l

Fill-in-the-blank
1. colossal
2. zany
3. lavish
4. puny
5. fraud
6. petty
7. accumulate
8. meandered
9. nausea
10. buffoon

Super Challenge
Answers will vary.

List #12, Answer Key

Matching
1. i
2. m
3. d
4. n
5. l
6. k
7. c
8. b
9. f
10. j

Bonus Words
11. o
12. g

Fill-in-the-blank
1. permeated
2. voracious
3. repertoire
4. reiterate
5. begrudging
6. pacifist
7. omniscient
8. animosity
9. superfluous
10. morose

Super Challenge
Answers will vary.

List #13, Answer Key

Matching
1. j
2. i
3. m
4. n
5. g
6. o
7. f
8. c
9. b
10. a

Bonus Words
11. k
12. e

Super Challenge
Answers will vary.

Fill-in-the-blank
1. ambitious
2. demented
3. frugal
4. haggled
5. bigot
6. subsequent
7. sparse
8. essential
9. wager
10. enchanted

List #14, Answer Key

Matching
1. m
2. j
3. n
4. l
5. d
6. i
7. a
8. b
9. f
10. e

Bonus Words
11. o
12. k

Super Challenge
Answers will vary.

Fill-in-the-blank
1. sprawled
2. lenient
3. envious
4. heathen
5. zest
6. anonymous
7. bungle
8. nimble
9. enhance
10. sieve

List #15, Answer Key

Matching	**Fill-in-the-blank**
1. m	1. nuptial
2. n	2. fluctuate
3. i	3. commend
4. c	4. pompous
5. h	5. authoritarian
6. o	6. chic
7. g	7. indigent
8. d	8. pilfered
9. a	9. dormant
10. f	10. expletive

Bonus Words

11. k
12. j

Super Challenge

Answers will vary.

List #16, Answer Key

Matching	**Fill-in-the-blank**
1. l	1. bedraggled
2. k	2. whim
3. b	3. jeopardy
4. a	4. adjacent
5. o	5. clamored
6. g	6. temperamental
7. c	7. menacing
8. d	8. synonymous
9. h	9. preliminary
10. j	10. pious

Bonus Words

11. e
12. i

Super Challenge

Answers will vary.

List #17, Answer Key

Matching

1. n
2. g
3. h
4. l
5. o
6. m
7. j
8. i
9. f
10. c

Bonus Words

11. b
12. d

Fill-in-the-blank

1. priority
2. retort
3. martyr
4. smattering
5. equivalent
6. haughty
7. notorious
8. obliterated
9. lacerated
10. degraded

Super Challenge

Answers will vary.

List #18, Answer Key

Matching

1. l
2. o
3. c
4. h
5. m
6. e
7. f
8. k
9. n
10. i

Bonus Words

11. j
12. a

Fill-in-the-blank

1. inoculated
2. shrewder
3. alleged
4. sabotage
5. pragmatic
6. exclusive
7. heterogeneous
8. homogeneous
9. evolved
10. bilked

Super Challenge

Answers will vary.

List #19, Answer Key

Matching
1. o
2. e
3. m
4. b
5. l
6. d
7. i
8. j
9. n
10. a

Bonus Words
11. c
12. g

Fill-in-the-blank
1. loquacious
2. incessantly
3. admonished
4. vile
5. conventional
6. passe
7. perusing
8. conjecture
9. extricate
10. vendetta

Super Challenge
Answers will vary.

List #20, Answer Key

Matching
1. l
2. j
3. e
4. c
5. h
6. d
7. k
8. n
9. m
10. b

Bonus Words
11. f
12. a

Fill-in-the-blank
1. impaired
2. vital
3. teetotalers
4. fanatics
5. competent
6. exasperate
7. ambidextrous
8. ample
9. reconciled
10. memento

Super Challenge
Answers will vary.

List #21, Answer Key

Matching
1. g
2. o
3. h
4. d
5. k
6. a
7. n
8. c
9. i
10. l

Bonus Words
11. b
12. m

Fill-in-the-blank
1. astounded
2. deemed
3. inhospitable
4. livid
5. irrational
6. reputable
7. squabble
8. sauteing
9. tweaked
10. elude

Super Challenge
Answers will vary.

List #22, Answer Key

Matching
1. j
2. b
3. k
4. d
5. c
6. o
7. l
8. a
9. g
10. f

Bonus Words
11. m
12. h

Fill-in-the-blank
1. veteran
2. poached
3. revive
4. competitor
5. windfall
6. gorging
7. rookie
8. molten
9. potential
10. sincere

Super Challenge
Answers will vary.

List #23, Answer Key

Matching
1. h
2. n
3. c
4. b
5. m
6. o
7. a
8. k
9. i
10. d

Bonus Words
11. j
12. f

Fill-in-the-blank
1. celebrity
2. edible
3. aromatic
4. bland
5. envious
6. lurking
7. cringed
8. brawl
9. jaunt
10. nurture

Super Challenge
Answers will vary.

List #24, Answer Key

Matching
1. k
2. e
3. d
4. h
5. c
6. m
7. o
8. l
9. f
10. j

Bonus Words
11. i
12. g

Fill-in-the-blank
1. immigrant
2. heritage
3. distinguished
4. partial
5. legible
6. staff
7. slogan
8. snide
9. feeble
10. underdog

Super Challenge
Answers will vary.

To Order

Please send me _____ copies of *AbraVocabra* and _____ copies of *More AbraVocabra*. I am enclosing $21.95 for each book ordered, plus shipping and handling ($4.50 for one book, $2.00 for each additional book). Colorado residents add 66¢ sales tax, per book. Total amount $_____.

Name _____

School _____
(Include only if using school address.)

Address _____

City _____ State _____ Zip Code _____

Method of Payment:

❑ Payment enclosed ❑ Visa/MC/Discover ❑ Purchase Order

Credit Card# _____Expiration Date _____

Signature _____

Send to:

Cottonwood Press, Inc.
107 Cameron Drive
Fort Collins, CO 80525
1-800-864-4297
www.cottonwoodpress.com

**Or call for a free catalog of practical materials
for English and language arts, grades 5-12.**

COTTONWOOD PRESS INC.